Celebration

THE LITURGY HANDBOOK

*

Edited by Stephen Dean

*

GEOFFREY
CHAPMAN

Geoffrey Chapman
A Cassell imprint
Villiers House, 41/47 Strand, London WC2N 5JE
387 Park Avenue South, New York, NY 10016–8810

© the editor and contributors 1993

First published 1993

British Library Cataloguing-in-Publication Data
A catalogue record for this book is available from the British Library.

Library of Congress Cataloging-in-Publication Data
Applied for.

ISBN 0–225–66692–8

Designed by John Leath, MSTD

Typeset by Intype, London

Printed and bound in Great Britain
by Biddles Ltd, Guildford and King's Lynn

CONTENTS

FOREWORD

I welcome very warmly the publication of this book. Even thirty years after the Council, liturgical information is still a very great need in our country and elsewhere. We need to have a better grasp and understanding of liturgical principles, which will in turn improve the level and quality of liturgical celebrations.

We are very blessed that many of those who have contributed to this book play an important part in liturgical formation at both national and local level. They speak therefore out of their own experience and share with us concerning the theological, pastoral and practical aspects of the Church's liturgy. May this book be a means of leading us to a greater awareness of what is at the heart of our celebration so that we may experience prayerful and inspiring liturgies.

✠ Thomas McMahon
Bishop of Brentwood
1 September 1993

THE CONTRIBUTORS

Unit 1   MICHAEL MULVIHILL

Michael Mulvihill cssp was ordained priest in 1966. He studied theology and liturgy in Rome for five years. After some years' teaching in Tanzania, he has been deeply involved in teaching and lecturing on liturgy, its theology and spirituality, in Ireland, the USA and Africa. He is at present on the staff of the Missionary Institute, London, and a member of the Committee for Pastoral Liturgy of the Bishops of England and Wales.

Unit 2   DEBORAH M. JONES

Deborah Jones trained as a teacher. Since 1980 she has been working as diocesan adviser for adult education in the diocese of East Anglia. She also lectures on religious subjects for Suffolk College and is Assistant Editor of the monthly journal *Priests and People*. As a member of the Liturgy Commission in that diocese, she has been responsible for the training of readers and ministers of communion. Her handbook *This Is My Body* (Kevin Mayhew, 1989), with workbooks for course participants, has become a standard text in several dioceses. An earlier book, *Focus on Faith*, also published by Kevin Mayhew, has run into several reprintings.

Unit 3   ALAN GRIFFITHS

Alan Griffiths is a priest of the diocese of Portsmouth. He studied at the English College in Rome and taught liturgy for six years at St John's Seminary, Wonersh. He serves on the Liturgy Commission of his own diocese and has served on the national Liturgy Committees.

Unit 4   JULIE ANNE DONNELLY

An Oxford graduate, trained as a geography teacher, Sister Julie Anne Donnelly worked for twenty years in secondary and tertiary education in Britain. She then spent three years in Rome in communications work for her congregation, the Sisters of Notre Dame of Namur, followed by almost seven years as press secretary to Cardinal Hume. Since obtaining a Diploma in Sacred Liturgy *cum laude* from the Irish Institute of Pastoral Liturgy, she has been involved in liturgical formation in the diocese of Plymouth, particularly by giving liturgy missions in the parishes. She is a member of the Plymouth diocesan Liturgy Commission.

Unit 5   PETER GALLACHER

Peter Gallacher has been Director of Liturgy for the past seven years at Chesters College near Glasgow. As secretary of the Scottish national Liturgy Commission he has been responsible for organizing two national Summer Schools on RCIA. He is at present the co-ordinator of a working party set up by the Bishops' Conference of Scotland to examine the Christian Initiation of children with a view to producing a new strategy for the future.

Unit 6   ROBIN GIBBONS

Robin Gibbons OSB is a priest working in the diocese of Portsmouth, and at present teaching liturgy at Wonersh and Heythrop College. He joined the Benedictines at Farnborough in 1972 and studied at Canterbury and Heythrop, where he gained his MTh.

He is a member of various liturgical societies and commissions including the Bishops' Committees for Art, Architecture and Heritage and the Portsmouth diocesan Liturgy Committee, and an advisor for *Church Building* magazine. He has lectured and written extensively in this field and is currently completing his doctorate in liturgical art and architecture.

Unit 7   STEPHEN DEAN

Stephen Dean became interested in liturgy when at junior seminary; he subsequently studied at the English College, Rome, but left before ordination. Since then he has worked in publishing and liturgical music. He worked at the St Thomas More Centre for Pastoral Liturgy for several years from its founding in 1969. He was also diocesan director of music (the first in the country) for the Arundel and Brighton diocese from 1979 to 1985. He is currently music advisor to the diocese of East Anglia and a member of the English and Welsh Bishops' Church Music Committee.

Unit 8   PAULINE CLARKE

Sister Pauline Clarke studied theology and liturgy in Rome. On returning to England she took up an appointment at Ushaw College, Durham, and then at the Missionary Institute, London, where she lectured in liturgy for ten years. The Prayer of the Church is her specialized field; she has given sessions to many religious communities and written a number of articles on the topic.

She has also lectured in liturgy in Jerusalem. At present she is liturgy adviser for the Northern Area of the Archdiocese of Westminster and a member of the working party currently engaged in the adaptation of the Prayer of the Church for use in parishes. Sister Pauline is also a member of the Pastoral Liturgy Committee of the Bishops' Conference of England and Wales.

Unit 9   J. D. CRICHTON

James Dunlop Crichton (b. 1907; ordained 1932; Prelate of Honour 1980) has served various parishes in the Birmingham archdiocese including Pershore (1955–77). Engaged in the liturgical movement years before Vatican II, he has lectured in various places in the UK, Ireland, the USA, Canada and Belgium. He has always been concerned to link liturgy with life. This is apparent in his trilogy *Christian Celebration: Understanding the Mass, the Sacraments* and *the Prayer of the Church* (revised editions, 1992–3).

Unit 10   TONY ROGERS

Tony Rogers is a priest of the diocese of East Anglia and was ordained in 1971. His ministry has been wholly parochial but he also serves on the national Pastoral Liturgy Committee and on the diocesan Liturgy Commission, as well as being Catholic adviser to Anglia TV. In recent years his special interest involved him in the adaptation of the Order of Christian Funerals for England, Wales and Scotland.

INTRODUCTION

The central importance of liturgy in the Church, and its changing shape during this century, especially since the Second Vatican Council, have stimulated an increasing interest in its how and why. This book is based on the Syllabus of Liturgical Formation published by the Bishops' Conference of England and Wales; but its presentation of various aspects of worship will, it is hoped, interest and inspire anyone wishing to develop an informed understanding of the liturgy.

The idea of a Liturgical Syllabus was mooted at the 1989 National Liturgical Conference in Cardiff. In the 1970s and 1980s there was more than one attempt to set up a National Liturgical Institute for England and Wales, or at least some national formation programme with its own staff, but although these schemes reached an advanced stage of planning they never received final episcopal approval. As an Institute therefore seemed to be off the agenda for the time being, the Syllabus was conceived as a way of providing at least *some* national guidance on liturgical formation, an urgent need in view of the growing demand from lay people for information and study on the liturgy. The suggestion came from Jennifer Demolder, who was acting Secretary of the Bishops' Committees, and was taken up with enthusiasm.

An *ad hoc* Formation Subcommittee with a member from each of the three committees on the liturgy (Pastoral Liturgy, Art and Architecture, and Music) met in late 1989 under the chairmanship of Bishop McMahon to decide on the work to be done. In early 1990 an outline draft of a syllabus, containing nine units, was drawn up and individual units were assigned to experts in the field to work on.

The content of the Syllabus was presented at a working week at Plater College, Oxford, in July 1990, and discussed by a group of fifty delegates representing most of the dioceses of England and Wales. The drafts were re-written in the light of comments made at that meeting; one of the units was subdivided, to make a total of ten.

The bishops of the Department for Christian Life and Worship approved the Syllabus in principle at their meeting in November 1990, and on 30 September 1991 it was published as *Celebrating the Paschal Mystery*, for an initial trial period of two years.

As its Foreword says, this Syllabus should be seen as part of the movement of liturgical formation required by Vatican II:

> The Church earnestly desires that all the faithful be led to that full, conscious, and active participation in liturgical celebrations called for by the very nature of the liturgy. Such participation by the Christian people as 'a chosen race, a royal priesthood, a holy nation, God's own people' (1 Peter 2:9; see 2:4–5) is their right and duty by reason of their baptism.
>
> In the reform and promotion of the liturgy, this full and active participation by all the people is the aim to be considered before all else. For it is the primary and indispensable source from which the faithful are to derive the true Christian spirit and therefore pastors must zealously strive in all their pastoral work to achieve such participation by means of the necessary instruction. (Liturgy Constitution, *Sacrosanctum Concilium* (SC), 14)

For many people, the changes in the liturgy which came about as a result of the Council were imposed rather than understood. To this day, there are many people who lived through that period who have never had the *reasons* for the changes explained to them. Far from the period of liturgical reform being over, then, it is still in progress, and will not have finished until knowledge of the reformed rites and their rationale has caught up with their actual usage. Into this situation comes the Syllabus, which provides, in the form of a series of topics and notes, the framework for a programme of study. It is not a worked-out study course, but a core syllabus which can be developed and used at a variety of levels. The principal agencies for its implementation are the Diocesan Liturgy Commissions, but any parish or group is free to use it. The adaptation of the Syllabus to take account of local needs, pastoral circumstances, and above all, the background and experience of the participants, is most important. Various ways of using it are suggested, such as a home-study course under the direction of a tutor, or parish or deanery sessions.

This book is the first to provide a worked-out programme of study specifically based on the Syllabus. It has been written by some of the most distinguished liturgists at work today in Britain, who are in many cases the people who originally compiled the units of the Syllabus. It is offered in the hope that it will prove valuable to those wishing to study the liturgy, either as individuals or because they exercise a liturgical ministry in their parishes or communities. It follows the layout of each unit quite closely, to allow it to be used either as a reading book or as the basis for a course of lectures. It aims at the average reader, not the liturgical specialist or the absolute novice.

The Foreword to the Syllabus includes an observation which should be warmly endorsed:

> It should be emphasised that the aim of this syllabus and any study course based on it is not the mere imparting of knowledge. Worship is action and commitment, and the purpose of acquiring an informed understanding of the liturgy should be to lead people into a renewed experience of prayer and to foster the practical skills needed in the community's worship.

STEPHEN DEAN

BASIC BIBLIOGRAPHY

(a) DOCUMENTS

The Constitution on the Liturgy of the Second Vatican Council, *Sacrosanctum Concilium* (SC) is essential reading for all parts of the Syllabus.

Austin Flannery (ed.), *Documents of the Second Vatican Council* (2 vols; Dublin: Dominican Publications, 1975/Leominster: Fowler Wright Books, 1981) contains the above Constitution and some other subsequent liturgical documents.

ICEL (ed.), *Documents on the Liturgy 1963–1979: Conciliar, Papal and Curial Texts* (Collegeville, MN: The Liturgical Press, 1982). Very detailed; a valuable work of reference.

The Liturgy Documents: A Parish Resource (Chicago: Liturgy Training Publications, 1992). Contains the fundamental liturgical documents in a handy format, with background notes. Also contains the (outstanding) US Bishops' documents on environment and art, and music. A useful and practical book.

C. J. Walsh (ed.), *Instructions on the Revised Roman Rites* (London: Collins, 1979). Parts of this collection is now out of date, or will be soon; but still a useful source.

(b) GENERAL WORKS

The following works cover most of the ground of the Syllabus.

J. D. Crichton, *Christian Celebration* (3 vols): *Understanding the Mass* (new edition 1992), *Understanding the Sacraments* (new edition 1993) and *Understanding the Prayer of the Church* (new edition 1993) (all London: Geoffrey Chapman).

Jean Lebon, *How to Understand the Liturgy* (London: SCM Press, 1987).

A. G. Martimort (ed.), *The Church at Prayer* (new edition, 4 vols; London: Geoffrey Chapman, 1986–8).

James L. White, *Introduction to Christian Worship* (Nashville, TN: Abingdon Press, 1980). An ecumenical work. Very useful.

Donald A. Withey, *Catholic Worship: An Introduction to Liturgy* (Bury St Edmunds: Kevin Mayhew, 1990). Suitable as a course book.

The series *American Essays in Liturgy* (Washington, DC: The Pastoral Press) is strongly recommended.

ABBREVIATIONS

APCS	Anointing and Pastoral Care of the Sick
DOL	*Documents on the Liturgy*
GILH	General Instruction on the Liturgy of the Hours
GIRM	General Instruction on the Roman Missal
GNLYC	General Norms for the Liturgical Year and the Calendar
ICEL	International Commission on English in the Liturgy
LG	*Lumen Gentium* (Constitution on the Church)
OCF	Order of Christian Funerals
OCM	Order of Christian Marriage
RCIA	Rite of Christian Initiation of Adults
SC	*Sacrosanctum Concilium* (Constitution on the Sacred Liturgy)

Unit 1

MICHAEL MULVIHILL CSSp

INTRODUCTION AND FOUNDATIONS

I. Introduction: Vatican II and the renewal of the liturgy

On 4 December 1963 the Constitution on the Sacred Liturgy, *Sacrosanctum Concilium* (SC) was promulgated. This event has brought great blessings on the Church, in particular a fresh realization of what God has done for us in the Paschal Mystery, Christ's saving passage from death to the fullness of life with God for ever.

This book takes the Liturgy Constitution as its starting point, and reflects on its teaching, principles and guidelines in the light of the considerable developments of the subsequent three decades.

The liturgical renewal has not been without its critics, but their criticisms have had the positive result of inspiring deeper reflection on the place of the liturgy in God's plan of salvation, and its fundamental importance in the life and mission of the Church.

Pope John Paul II, in his letter to commemorate the twenty-fifth anniversary of the promulgation of the Constitution, made a powerful plea for continuing biblical and liturgical formation (15): 'The most urgent task is that of the biblical and liturgical formation of the people of God, both pastors and faithful ... This is a long-term programme ... A formation suitable to their state is indispensable also for lay people.'

1. Why was reform of the liturgy necessary?

The Constitution's publication stimulated a profound exploration of the reasons for such a comprehensive renewal and promotion. It was something new in the life of the Western Catholic Church. It is true that the Church always drew on its liturgical tradition, but this tradition had been long forgotten in ordinary parish life and in spiritual writings. The new situation called for intensive efforts at re-education.

The fundamental reason for the liturgical reform could be briefly stated thus: as a result of the work of the liturgical movement, liturgy came to be understood as a primarily theological reality. Rather than being seen in juridical or ceremonial categories, liturgy came to be appreciated as a gift coming from God the Father to his Church, as revealing God's purpose, as containing and manifesting the work of salvation, as the source and goal of the whole life of the Church. From this fundamental statement follows the realization that liturgy belongs to the order of faith, prior to any artistic, cultural or other considerations. Liturgy is the celebration of the faith of the Church.

A reading of the main theological articles of SC (2; 5–8; 10) gives us the framework within which to understand the word 'liturgy'. SC 7 offers something like a definition of the liturgy, and it is a very valuable one. But such formulae, seen in isolation, are incomplete. To complete them one has to enter the culture or world of meaning of the liturgy, from which it derives its character and purpose. This may involve a conversion of perspective and outlook.

Any adequate vision of liturgy must include at least the following elements:

- God's graceful and merciful initiative
- the history of salvation which reaches its fullness in the Christian Gospel
- the coming together of God's people to celebrate his glory in praise and thanksgiving
- God's revelation of himself in Christ's presence in the celebration which is structured
    - through believers gathered in the fellowship of the Holy Spirit,
    - through word proclaimed,
    - through sacrament or ritual carried out
- participation in mission which arises from participation in God's saving work – the Paschal Mystery – present in the liturgical celebration.

It must be constantly emphasized that liturgy is sacramental, symbolic and ritual in character. Since these words may have negative associations, it is vital, at an early stage of study of liturgy, to grasp their importance. Any study course that does not teach Christians the language of sacrament and symbol is gravely inadequate. The lack of such help in the past may explain the 'foreign' character that Christian worship has for many contemporary Christians.

A clear vision of the unity and harmony of the above elements is a spur to making such wealth available to the whole Church. The great figures of the liturgical movement clearly perceived that the liturgy thus understood pertains to the very nature of the Church. Ultimately, liturgical reform emerged from a renewed vision of the Church's faith, which is something that has to be celebrated by the whole community of baptized believers.

It was evident in the earlier part of the twentieth century that the language, rites, texts, style and spirit of the liturgy did not easily make visible the mystery it contained, nor did liturgical law and practice encourage that active participation in faith and love which the Council, following a text of Pope Pius X, declares to be the 'primary and indispensable source of the true Christian spirit' (SC 14). In fact, the attitudes of most of the clergy and laity were far removed from such a vision, and the change of ritual and language had to be accompanied by a change of attitude and faith perception.

The promotion of liturgical renewal is nothing less than procla-mation of the gospel of salvation in sacramental form, to bring human beings to the fullness of communion with the God whose glory is both manifested and celebrated in the worship he has given us in Christ (SC 5; 43).

2. What did it seek to achieve?

The Constitution itself explains its purpose. It has a comprehensive vision which sees that the overall renewal of the Church is intimately linked with the liturgy, and especially with active participation in it (cf. SC 14).

The frequent and regular celebration of the liturgy, above all follow-ing closely the unfolding of the Paschal Mysery in the liturgical year, brings believers into intimate communion with the living heart of Christian existence. Liturgical celebration is the origin, the centre, the climax of the being and mission of Church. Through liturgy the Church becomes more fully itself, for it is by vocation and divine designation the community of worship (cf. SC 5; 26; 41).

The key to appreciating this is the insight of faith that God, Father, Son and Holy Spirit, is truly present and acting when the Church gathers in the name of the Lord Jesus, risen in glory, and when it proclaims the living Word and celebrates the rites and symbols called sacraments. In short, what the Council hoped to achieve through reform and promotion of liturgy is what the liturgy itself is about. The more we enter into the culture of liturgy the more we become what God wants us to be.

3. What were the principles by which the reform was to be carried out?

The Syllabus lists (pp. 9–10) the main principles of reform enunciated by the Liturgy Constitution. Those who have worked to implement the reform have based their projects on these principles, as a reading of the General Instruction on the Roman Missal (GIRM), for example, will amply show.

Any attempt to enter fruitfully into the culture of the liturgy must give priority to the Bible, the meaning of the Church in God's plan and the principle of authenticity of sign and text, so that the Mystery of Christ, present in a hidden way in the liturgical celebration, may be clearly manifested through the signs and symbols (cf. SC 21).

The principles on which the reform is based are also the principles which constitute the Liturgy itself.

4. What is the Council's understanding and vision?

The Council's understanding and vision is expressed in the whole of the Liturgy Constitution, read and interpreted in the context of all the Council documents. This interpretative framework should include the receptive process of the post-Conciliar Church. 'Reception' is the technical term for the Spirit-guided discernment by which the whole Church acknowledges the truth of official statements and begins to live by them.

A great help to understanding the Council's vision is found in the writings of Dom Odo Casel OSB, who devoted his life to exploring the principles of liturgical renewal, above all the Paschal Mystery. It was his disciples who were most influential in the writing of the Liturgy Constitution.

The occasional difficulties in the implementation of the Constitution may be explained in some measure by a failure to recognize the vision of the Council and accept the enrichment and change of outlook that it implies. The most concentrated statement of this vision is in the doctrinal statements of the documents, the most important of which are SC 2, 5–8 and 10. The Council provides a new framework, even a new culture of faith, to help us to be at home in the world of the liturgy, and new 'eyes' to see the significance of the signs, whether texts or rites, as they reveal to believing participants the mystery they contain. By pondering on the text of the Constitution in the light of frequent celebration (the best way of studying the liturgy), Christians will come to perceive that the liturgy is the great teacher of faith because it is the presence of him in whom we believe, and the presence of all he did for our salvation.

SC 5–8 form a powerful commentary on the meaning and purpose of liturgical celebration. These articles offer us a vision of God's graceful initiative and action which form the history of salvation. By assimilating the overall vision we are enabled to acquire the liturgical mind, which is nothing other than the mind of faith and the Church.

Some points to further study are these:

- the Trinitarian structure of the plan of salvation
- the historical dynamic: it begins with God's free and graceful initiative, moves through Israel's history and reaches its fullest manifestation in Christ and his work of salvation, the Paschal Mystery which is the very content of right worship (SC 5)
- the plan of salvation is continued in the power of the Spirit through the Church and its history, and is made actual when the Church meets for worship (SC 6)
- these meetings are called liturgical celebrations; in them Christ is truly present and acting in a variety of ways so that they are the actions of Christ–Church; as such they are the most important actions of the Church (SC 7)
- the liturgy on earth is a participation in the liturgy of heaven which is the goal and completion of the journey of the pilgrim Church (SC 8)

The vision of the Council is a challenge for us, even now. It may clash with the expectations of many Catholics who have not yet discovered it. This can be a painful struggle, calling for a different understanding of God and his gracious approach to us in those epiphanies of his that we call liturgical celebrations.

II: Foundations

The Syllabus approaches this central topic by moving from the general phenomenon of human worship to the specific nature of Christian worship.

This is a common method in today's increasingly secular-minded and humanistic society. However, it has to be made explicit that while Christian worship has its human aspects, it is founded on God's revelation. What is specifically Christian comes uniquely from God as his gracious gift to his Church (SC 5). For the same reason, Christian worship can only be understood and appreciated by people with the priceless gift of faith. This faith is not an occasional personal act or something marginal to everyday existence: it is a whole way of thinking, acting and living.

Why do people worship? If it were merely an activity arising out of human need, we would have to explain why huge numbers of people do not worship, and some publicly attack it. There are apostles of atheism. The Liturgy Constitution makes it clear that Christian worship arises out of the coming of the eternal Word made flesh who accomplished the Paschal Mystery in obedience to his Father's purpose: 'Thus in Christ there came forth the perfect satisfaction needed for our reconciliation, and we receive the means for giving worthy worship to God' (SC 5; cf. what the Dogmatic Constitution on Divine Revelation (1965) has to say about the revelation–faith relationship (2–6)).

The approach by way of human need can, however, alert Christians to the value of ritual and symbol, which is in harmony with the incarnational style of God's communication with human beings, usually called the sacramental principle. The Paschal Mystery is something totally new in the relationship between God and humanity. It demands a complete change of direction in human history. It inspires a wholly new way of understanding God, the human person, social relationships, the future of the human race. The Church, which emerges from the Paschal Mystery, is the community of ongoing conversion and initiation into true Christian worship.

Only God can demand genuine conversion. Hence, God's Word must be the constant companion of the Christian. Indeed, the Church, above all in worship, may be described as the school of the Word, or the forum where the dialogue of salvation takes place. God begins this dialogue and we hear him in the Scriptures proclaimed and read in prayer, in the rites of the Church – blessings, exorcisms, anointings and other ritual actions and gestures – and, primarily, in the sacraments.

Peter Fink writes: 'Ritual engages people in a network of signifying activity, the very doing of which involves them in a new way of feeling and acting as well as understanding.' Rites, symbols and sacraments are in their own particular mode genuine means of communication between God and his people. One could say, in short, that God's communication with human beings is ritual and sacramental. Rituals address the whole person and draw us into the plan and purpose of God. We use them as points of reference because of their Gospel-given significance; they are in their own way the Gospel proposed to us, and they mould us in the manner of the Gospel they celebrate.

Rituals make us do and say certain things, which change us in the very act of using them. Mark Searle writes: 'The words and gestures of the rite bring us to stand at the end of human action and language, till we tremble on the edge of that ultimately unnameable and unmanageable mystery we call God.' The very doing of the rites and words reorders our standing and relationship with the community to which we belong. They mediate social life, and our identity is established in social relationships. But they also, in line with the incarnation and in the power of the Holy Spirit, mediate the mystery of God, which goes beyond our capacity to understand and express.

All this explains why liturgy contains so many rites, gestures and symbols: they are part of its *sacramentality*. It also explains why catechesis is not simply the imparting of information but, while including this, must also be a global experience of the life of the Christian community. Believing people, the Word of God, a multitude of rites and symbols, all combine to provide an environment of conversion–repentance–faith that leads to an intense experience of the Paschal Christ. This reaches a marvellous manifestation in the night of Easter, when the history of salvation is retold and the elect are bathed in water, anointed with sweet-smelling chrism, dressed in brilliant white robes and come, holding lighted candles, around the table of the Lord to eat and drink the body and blood of the risen Lord in whom they have been incorporated.

Symbols are difficult for people of a technological turn of mind to appreciate. Materialism is a hindrance to the appreciation of the transcendence of God and the spiritual nature of human beings. However, it can bring home the reality of the incarnation, in which the material world is used by the Holy Spirit to further the new creation of the Risen One. The Passover of Christ Jesus from death to life is the central event of human history. It is remembered and made present through the sacramental and ritual actions by which the saving work of the Blessed Trinity is mediated to human beings.

The principle of sacramentality, i.e., the mediation of Christian salvation through persons, words, actions and the elements of the cosmos, is so firmly held by the Catholic Church(es) that it is regarded as fundamental to their identity. The Christian community uses a complex (or forest) of symbols to speak about the Trinitarian God and the Word made flesh by the action of the Spirit in the womb of the Virgin Mary. These symbols also speak to enquiring believers about the meaning of the reality that they actually and effectively symbolize. They are legitimate and necessary objects of study.

These symbolic or sacramental actions do not exist in a vacuum. Nor is their sacramentality strictly limited to the precise points of bathing, hand-laying, anointing, offering, eating and drinking and so on. It is, so to speak, spread out through time. Ever since the Church has striven to understand its faith, and particularly its ritual celebration of that faith, there has been unanimous acceptance that these rites do contain the reality they celebrate. The Paschal Mystery is present and effective in liturgical celebrations through the power of the Holy Spirit

7

(cf., e.g., SC 7; 61). The symbols of the liturgy are manifestations of the saving activity of God, and thus, in their own way, revelations of God. They are *mysteries*, rooted in the New Testament understanding of 'mystery': cf. Ephesians 3:3–12; Colossians 1:24 – 2:3, 9–15.

Christian faith presents the meaning of the symbols as founded on the Incarnation. God spoke to and communicated with the human race through the (bodily/fleshly/material) humanity of his Son, the Word made flesh. Because of the Incarnation, the Word made flesh is the sacrament of all sacraments, or as recent theologians put it, Jesus is the primordial sacrament.

Liturgical rites are the social language by which the Church expresses its identity, creates its own environment and style and hands on its tradition of gospel, life and worship. The observance of the rites of the Church is a primary way in which *mission* is actualized. They are the cement that holds the Church together.

The Bible is the written record of the plan or history of salvation. The relationship between word and symbolic action forms an intimate unity, giving rise to the unity of the act of sacramental worship (SC 56). Similarly, the symbols and rites of the liturgy derive their meaning from the history of salvation, centred on the Paschal Mystery, and thus from the Bible, the means of most fully interpreting the Paschal Mystery (Luke 24:13–35). 'It is from Scripture that actions and signs derive their meaning' (SC 24). We are happy today to acknowledge that these symbols do (in their own way) truly mediate the Paschal Mystery (SC 6; 60; 61).

A description of 'symbol' might be this:

> A symbol stands for another reality, but it reveals that reality in its own structure. Of its nature it is limited, but it reveals a reality that goes beyond the limits of the symbol itself. The task of a symbol is to make the transcendent or some aspect of the transcendent available and to mediate participation in that which is revealed... It is the sensible expression of the transcendent; as such it is the place of revelation and of participation in that which is revealed. Symbols invite us to come to terms with their meaning, they challenge us to inhabit their world... In a sense, then, symbols are open-ended. By engaging in symbols, by inhabiting their world, people discover new meanings, new values, new motivations, new horizons for their lives... Their relation to people is reciprocal in the sense that they disclose new potentials for human life but they also are shaped and refined or even distorted by the changing circumstances of life. (Seasoltz)

A description of 'rite' might be this:

> A ritual is basically a complexus of structured symbols ... Ritual
> is above all repetitive behaviour. It has to do with recurring
> symbols which support and elicit recurring responses. (Seasoltz)

The term 'celebration' is used in contemporary liturgical books and
theology in a special sense, somewhat different from the everyday one.
Usually *celebration* has to do with festivity, the natural human reaction
on the arrival of good news. In the contemporary liturgical sense,
celebration includes the following:

- a gathering of the People of God
- to participate today in the Mystery of Christ present by way of the
  ritual of word proclaimed and heard and sacrament or symbol
  enacted and shared
- the rhythm and dynamic of the liturgical year
- remembrance of all that God has done for humanity and its salvation
- looking forward to the completion of all things in God's good time
- giving thanks and praise to God for his blessings given to us in
  Christ, acknowledging his glory in beauty and holiness
- making intercession that the purpose of God may be fulfilled in the
  celebrants and, through them, in the world.

It is at the heart of the Christian understanding of celebration that
Christ is present in the liturgical act and effects his work of salvation
through the gathering and its rituals, associating the assembly with
himself in his ceaseless worship of our Father in the fellowship of the
Holy Spirit (cf. SC 7).

Christian celebration is made up of three integral elements, as indicated in SC 6:

- the coming together of believers in response to the apostolic
  announcement of God's redeeming work in Christ
- the proclamation of the Scriptures
- the celebration of the eucharist (or other sacrament or ritual)

To sum up, God's grace is his work of salvation given freely to the
whole human race, for their joyful and grateful acceptance. Liturgical
celebration is the 'work of our redemption' (SC 2, LG 3) mediated by
the Church's rituals. To celebrate is to carry out and participate in
these saving rituals in faith and worshipful praise and thanksgiving.

- Liturgical celebrations contain the Paschal Mystery of human sal-

9

vation, and mediate it through assembly, word proclaimed and sacrament, symbol and ritual (cf. SC 7).

- Liturgical celebrations are visible signs of God's gracious love and mercy communicated through the Word who became flesh, the sacrament of God.
- Liturgical celebrations are sacramental actualizations, in a ritual manner, of God's self-revelation.

Just as the purpose of God's self-revelation is to summon all humanity into communion with himself, so the purpose of liturgical celebration is, through affirming God's glory, to bring the participants together in the Trinitarian communion of the Church, sacrament of the presence of the Father, Son and Holy Spirit in the world.

The Paschal Mystery

At the heart of any investigation into the meaning of liturgy is the question: Who is God? How do we know him? We answer: by God's *revelation* in and through Jesus of Nazareth. Jesus is known to us as *Saviour*; God is revealed as the saving God. Liturgical celebrations are manifestations, revelations, apparitions and actualizations of God's saving activity in Christ's Paschal Mystery.

By revelation we know also that God is the Creator, and therefore Saviour, of all humanity; he acts in various ways, open or hidden, to draw all human beings to himself. This calls for some sense of history on our part since history is the stage for this ceaseless relationship between God and the human race.

One people became profoundly conscious that they had been specially chosen by God: the people of Israel. They saw certain events in their history as due to God's intervention. God saved them and made a covenant with them to which he was ever faithful in spite of their many sins and disloyalties. Events which had one meaning on the level of experience came, through the prophetic interpretation of history, to be seen as saving actions of Israel's God, forming part of the *history of salvation*. This prophetic interpretation is an essential component of any Christian effort to understand the faith and worship of the Church, the New Israel.

In due time, Jesus of Nazareth appeared among the people of Israel and proclaimed the coming of the Kingdom of God. Those who believed in him came to understand that he was sent by God, indeed was God's deputy, acting and speaking on behalf of God himself; he was recognized as God's very Son, equal to him in all things.

Jesus died and was raised from the dead. The more Christians reflected on the resurrection the more they came to realize that this event was the fulfilment of all the promises and hopes of Israel, indeed of all humanity. Soon they saw Jesus himself as the centre and Lord of all history, the hope and salvation of the human race.

By interpreting history in the light of the resurrection, they concluded that with the resurrection the rule of God had broken definitively into this world. We are now living in the last times; nothing radically different can now be expected from God in his relationship with us. God has made himself known to us as totally faithful to his promises; this means that there is more to human existence than everyday drudgery and the struggle to survive: a new light has shone on us by which we know that we have a surpassing worth and are destined for a glory beyond imagining.

The resurrection was so complete a revelation of God's glory and power that everything is governed by it; the future will be nothing other than the working out or flowering of the resurrection. All human beings are called to share in this newness of life; every person is offered the opportunity of participating in the victory of God over the most anti-human forces, those of death, sin and evil.

The Church arose out of this ultimate victory. It is not a social grouping of the followers of Jesus. It is rightly described and understood only as the *mystery* of the visible communion of the Father, the Son and the Holy Spirit in this world. The Church expresses its identity and mission by being faithful to its originating event, proclaiming it and celebrating it in the hope of the consummation of all things in its risen Lord.

Because Israel associated its salvation and origins with the Passover event and rituals of its people, and because the New Testament sets the death of Jesus in the framework of the Passover, the Church came to describe the work of salvation centred on Jesus' death and resurrection as *the Paschal Mystery*. The word 'mystery' is used especially in the letters to the Ephesians and the Colossians, and was translated by Tertullian as *sacramentum*. It has to do with God's plan, intention or purpose and can be understood as summing up the economy (i.e. plan) of salvation that is the person of Christ himself. Mystery, therefore, means the revelation, apparition, manifestation or epiphany of God's saving work and God's saving person, Jesus.

This outline indicates the chief elements needed to provide the context within which Christian liturgy makes sense. In a word, we can say: Christian liturgy is both the profession and the celebration of the Church's faith.

'Liturgy' and 'Paschal Mystery', therefore, are intimately linked. Some of these links can be explored:

1. The Paschal Mystery is God's action for our salvation accomplished

through the passage of his Son Jesus from this world to the fullness of life and glory. This work of salvation is brought to fulfilment in the course of history by the Holy Spirit which the Paschal Lord has poured out on the world and on his Church. Liturgy is the celebration of the Paschal Mystery. So liturgy is a theological reality, i.e., it has to do with God, who gives it meaning.

2. Liturgy makes use of the whole cluster of words and concept that we use to express our (admittedly limited) understanding of God and his involvement in human history. This explains the provisions of SC 15–19. The liturgy is an object of theological reflection, that is, we can discover something of God by reflecting on the liturgy.

3. To appreciate the liturgy we need to grow in faith, with particular attention to the Bible. The close following of the liturgical year is a means of great growth in faith-development, in which we enter the unfolding of the mystery of Christ. The liturgical year is indeed a *sacrament*, as in 'the Sacrament of Easter'.

4. Since all Christian life is dependent on the Paschal Mystery, it is centred on the liturgy which is the celebration of that mystery. All prayer and spirituality find in the liturgy their source and climax (cf. SC 10). Between the liturgy as revelation of God's saving work on the one hand, and contemplation on the other, there is the closest link.

A consequence of the realization that the liturgy is itself the Paschal work of salvation is that the former division of sacramental theology and liturgical studies is now being overcome. The fundamental statement must be something like this: God planned the salvation of human beings precisely in their humanity, and in his wisdom God sent his Son to be our incarnate Saviour. The liturgy therefore mediates that salvation (the Paschal Mystery) to human beings in human ways. Liturgical celebrations are profoundly adapted to the needs of human persons, who are themselves made in the image (sacrament) and likeness of God.

The elements that help towards an appreciation of the liturgical year are:

(a) The liturgical year is a memorial of the mystery of Christ the saving Lord in the course of time.

(b) In keeping the memorial of the Lord's saving work the Church makes present what we celebrate so that we may participate in it.

(c) The liturgical year is the celebration of the unfolding in time of the mystery of Christ.

(d) Through the close following of the liturgical year we meet the

Lord himself day by day, week by week, season by season, festival by festival.

(e) The Paschal Mystery of the Lord's death and resurrection is the foundation of the liturgical year, as it is of the entire life of the Church. It is because of this belief that we can see the primacy and importance of the Lord's Day or Sunday. What Sunday is for the week, Easter is for the whole year: the supreme festival.

The mystery of Christ and the Paschal Mystery are celebrated in full each day through the eucharist and the Liturgy of the Hours, but this celebration becomes more intensive and ritually fuller on certain days and during certain seasons. Among these Sunday has priority.

Sunday, the day of the Paschal Mystery: the resurrection as central event of history

The resurrection is the beginning of the new age, when we begin to wait in joyful hope for the coming of our saviour, Jesus Christ.

Out of the Paschal event springs forth the Church and its worship. The risen Lord commissions his disciples to baptize until the end of the world (Matthew 28:16–20). Paul witnesses to the Lord's Supper as being celebrated 'until the Lord comes again' (1 Corinthians 11:26). This perspective of expectation is understood as coming from the Lord himself when commanding 'do this in memory of me' (see, e.g., Luke 22:16, 18, 19).

The first communities understood the historical significance of the resurrection when they began to observe, not the Sabbath, but the 'first day of the week' (Mark 16:2; Matthew 28:1; Luke 24:1; John 20:1). This term expresses the sense of the new creation and looks forward to the consummation of all things (see Revelation 1:8, 10; 21: 1, 3, 6; 22:7, 12–13, 17, 20).

Christians gather in the name of Jesus at particular times, called globally 'the liturgical year', 'the year of salvation' or 'the year of the Lord'. The liturgical year is of the order of 'sacrament' or 'mystery', above all, through the celebration of Sunday, the Lord's Day. From a secular viewpoint Sunday is a day like any other, part of the weekend, rather than the 'first day of the week' with connotations of eternity and ultimate reality. But through our gatherings for worship, especially for the eucharist, Sunday takes on a particular meaning; Sunday is a sacrament.

The Liturgy Constitution, in three articles, gives high prominence to Sunday:

1. Article 6: 'From that time onwards the Church has never failed to come together to celebrate the Paschal Mystery.'

   (Note here the meaning of 'celebration', the content of which is the Paschal Mystery celebrated in time and the manner of which contains three integral elements:
   (a) gathering together as Church
   (b) reading the Scriptures
   (c) celebrating the eucharist.)
2. Article 102: here we find the key and fundamental notion of 'memorial';
   * the year and the work of salvation are brought together
   * Sunday is mentioned before even Easter itself.
3. Article 106: a magnificent statement of the deepest and most traditional meaning of Sunday:
   * Sunday is of apostolic tradition
   * it is rooted in the resurrection
   * it is the Church's celebration of the Paschal Mystery
   * it is the eighth day, a title used by the Fathers of the Church to suggest eternity
   * it is the day of the (risen/exalted) Lord, with eschatological connotations (a sign and pledge of that Day which is to come)
   * the manner of celebration is set out as in 6, though with greater richness
   * the primacy and centrality of the Sunday is stated: 'Hence the Lord's Day is the original feast day, and it should be proposed to the piety of the faithful and taught to them in such a way that it may become in fact a day of joy and freedom from work'
   * Sunday is the foundation and nucleus of the liturgical year and is indispensable to it.

The liturgical assembly

The document produced in 1991 by the Association of National Liturgy Secretaries of Europe, *Leading the Prayer of God's People*, makes this comprehensive statement:

> The liturgical assembly itself is the primary and most
> fundamental celebrant of liturgy. It is called together in order to
> carry out, in faith and in praise, its baptismal priestly ministry.
> When it is duly constituted, the assembly is the outstanding
> sign of the presence of Christ to his Church. (p. 1)

This echoes the fundamental text of GIRM:

The Lord's Supper or Mass gathers together the people of God, with a priest presiding in the person of Christ, to celebrate the memorial of the Lord or eucharistic sacrifice. For this reason the promise of Christ is particularly true of such a local congregation of the Church. 'Where two or three are gathered in my name, there am I in their midst' (Matthew 18:20). (GIRM 7)

It is to be noted about this text:

- the gathered people is the celebrating subject of the eucharist
- the local congregation is seen to be an integral part of the celebration of the eucharist
- the biblical text is an ecclesial one, 'gathered'
- Christ is present in the assembly itself.

These statements represent quite a revolution, and the teaching that Christ exercises his work of salvation and worship through his body, the whole community gathered in his name, needs constant emphasis. We must convey vividly the value of taking part in the common act of worship of the assembly of Christ. The visible gathering of the baptized is the sign, or even the sacrament, of the communion of the Triune God. So participation, communion and assembly are all closely connected.

Reading through GIRM, one is struck by how seriously and generously its authors took the principles of Vatican II, and indeed developed them.

Certain texts are immediately appropriate to our topic:

Everyone in the eucharistic assembly has the right and duty to take his own part according to the diversity of orders and functions. (GIRM 58)

In the celebration of Mass the faithful form a holy people, a chosen race, a royal priesthood: they give thanks to the Father and offer the victim not only through the hands of the priest but also with him, and they learn to offer themselves. They should make this clear by their deep sense of religion and their charity to everyone who shares in the celebration.

Any appearance of individualism or division among the faithful should be avoided, since they are all brothers and sisters in the sight of the one Father.

They should become one body, hearing the word of God, joining in prayers and song, and offering sacrifice and sharing the Lord's table together. This unity is especially evident in the common postures and actions observed by the faithful.

The people should serve willingly when asked to perform some particular ministry in the celebration. (GIRM 62)

This text speaks in its entirety of unity, communion, participation as a community, the role of individual members of the assembly.

In relation to the assembly it is fruitful to reflect on SC 7, one of the truly outstanding and enriching statements of Vatican II for its emphasis on the presence of the living Christ in the liturgy:

- It is the presence of Christ that makes the liturgical actions revelations of God, living events and efficacious experiences of salvation. This allows the Council to make statements whose implications some people have baulked at: 'every liturgical celebration ... is a sacred action surpassing all others'; 'the liturgy is the summit toward which the activity of the Church is directed; it is also the fount from which all her power flows'.
- This presence is purposeful; it is manifold in mode; it is ecclesial; it is sacramental/symbolic.
- Vatican II stands firmly and faithfully in the full Catholic tradition when it states that Paschal salvation is mediated effectively through 'sensible signs', i.e., through sacraments/symbols/liturgical actions, through material elements of the cosmos.
- The intimate union of Christ and the Church is a vital factor in the understanding of liturgy. When the Church worships it participates in Christ's own worship.
- In connection with the second reflection above it is of great interest that the single scripture text quoted in SC 7 is Matthew 18:20, which refers to the ecclesial presence of Christ. The significance of this will not escape the perceptive reader. It would appear that the presence of Christ in and to his gathered Church has a primary importance and methodological value.
- An especial reflection would address the text's analysis of the presence of Christ in the liturgical celebration. For the sake of clarity and to give the conciliar teaching its full impact let us set it out like this:

CHRIST IS PRESENT
in his Church
in its liturgical celebrations
in the sacrifice of the Mass
in the person of the minister
in the eucharistic species especially

in the sacraments
in the word proclaimed in Church
in the praying and singing of the Church

This text expresses the deepest nature of the liturgical celebration: its *saving* character. The reason for this, briefly, is that the risen and saving Lord Jesus is present and active in the whole of the liturgical celebration.

We are thus invited to experience liturgical *celebration* as the *presence* of the Lord Jesus. If we can successfully connect these two words we will enter more deeply into the world-view contained in the text.

Further thoughts can be derived from SC 7.

1. The meaning of liturgy. It is in the context of God's plan of salvation that liturgical celebrations make sense. They are the sacraments of God's saving work and purpose.
2. The ecclesial nature of the liturgical celebrations. Note the priority given in the text to the ecclesial presence of Christ, and the notion of the celebration as icon or expression of the Church.
3. The intimate union between Christ and his Church. The worship the Church offers is that of Christ himself.
4. The dignity, the worth and the value of liturgical celebrations is due to their status as actions of Christ–Church.
5. Liturgical celebration is of the order of sign, sacrament and symbol.
6. The presence of Christ in the liturgical celebrations makes them the reference point for the whole life of the Church.
7. To say that Christ is present in liturgical celebration is an act of faith.
8. The presence of the Lord will one day be experienced in glory as 'face to face', whereas now it is under the veil of sign, symbol, and sacrament. The fullness of presence is 'not yet'.
9. It is the Spirit who causes the risen Lord to be present and so gives life to the liturgical celebration.

Participation

Believers participate in the mystery (sacrament) by participating in the ritual of the communion of the Church. Through the rite we approach the mystery. It may be helpful to reflect on what many commentators consider the cardinal article (14) of the Liturgy Constitution. The text (in the Abbott edition) reads:

Mother Church earnestly desires that all the faithful be led to that full, conscious, and active participation in liturgical celebrations which is demanded by the very nature of the liturgy. Such participation by the Christian people as 'a chosen race, a royal priesthood, a holy nation, a purchased people' (1 Peter 2:9; cf. 2:4–5), is their right and duty by reason of their baptism.

In the restoration and promotion of the sacred liturgy, this full and active participation by all the people is the aim to be considered before all else; for it is the primary and indispensable source from which the faithful are to derive the true Christian spirit. Therefore, through the needed programme of instruction, pastors of souls must zealously strive to achieve it in all their pastoral work.

The Council then goes on to urge pastors to become filled with the spirit and power of the liturgy. It is evident that the text recognizes that, in 1963, this was far from being the case. Recent Roman documents indicate that the authorities do not think very much has changed. This text suggests the following reflections.

1. It is of the nature of liturgical celebration that all the baptized participate in it. A primary task of pastoral work is to help Christians develop a strong baptismal piety and spirituality. This would lead quickly to the realization, of major importance, that it is the whole assembly of baptized Christians which is the celebrant of the liturgy.
2. The called-for participation derives its content and shape from the celebration itself. Post-conciliar liturgical theology has extensively developed this aspect of the question.
3. Participation is characterized as being 'full, active, and conscious' (article 48 speaks of participation in the Mass as being 'knowing, devout, and active'). These qualities suggest what pastoral work should be aiming at.
4. The promotion of active participation has an absolute priority: 'before all else'.
5. Participation is connected very closely with the corporate nature of the liturgical act: it is the priestly, baptized people that carry out the act, and they do so as a community (cf. SC 2).
6. Active participation 'is the primary and indispensable source from which the faithful are to derive the true Christian spirit'.

The understanding of what participation means and demands has greatly increased in the years since 1963. Three New Testament texts will help to show how important and integral to the Christian vision this concept is.

TEXT 1: 1 JOHN 1:1–10. This text makes great use of the word *koinōnia*, whose importance has been emphasized in recent years. Modern translations variously use *fellowship* and *share* or *union*. *The New Jerome Biblical Commentary* (London: Geoffrey Chapman, 1989) opts for *fellowship*, but also refers to *partnership* and *communion* as translations for this word.

The use of *communion* opens up a new field, the ecclesiology of communion (i.e. the view of the Church as one single body) which, closely linked with eucharistic ecclesiology (the view of the Church as constituted by the eucharist), has had such an impact on liturgical spirituality in recent times.

This text offers us a very enriching framework for understanding the concept of participation, which embraces such ideas as:

- revelation
- apostolic witness and proclamation
- Trinitarian communion
- ecclesial unity
- moral behaviour
- Christ's work of paschal salvation
- realism about the human need of salvation and cleansing from sin.

These points provide us with some of the elements needed for recognizing the importance of participation in liturgical celebration. It is clear that the ecclesiology of communion underlies SC 14.

TEXT 2: 1 CORINTHIANS 10:16–17. This text is both ecclesiological and eucharistic. It will be even more rewarding if read also as a liturgical text, as a ritual text, even as a rubrical directive with a powerful theological and soteriological content.

> The cup of blessing that we bless, is it not a sharing in the blood of Christ? The bread that we break, is it not a sharing in the body of Christ? Because there is one bread, we who are many are one body, for we all partake of the one bread.

The following comments may be made:

- St Paul is describing and interpreting the ritual action of the eucharist with which his readers are familiar
- he understands the body of Christ in two senses, one sacramental, the other ecclesiological
- the connection between the two is by way of sharing, i.e. the ritual action of eating together the broken bread, illustrating the axiom

made popular in this century by Cardinal de Lubac: 'The Church makes the Eucharist; the Eucharist makes the Church'
• the meaning of the ritual eating of the broken bread is 'sharing' and 'partaking'.

This text, in short, enables us to see the close connection between *eucharist, Church, local church* or *assembly, ritual* and *participation*. It also draws attention to the ritual of the breaking of the bread, which has been given an immense importance by the liturgical reform (see GIRM 48,3; 56, 56c; 283).

TEXT 3: 1 CORINTHIANS 11:23–26. This is St Paul's account of the eucharist, probably as celebrated in his churches. We limit our comment to verse 26, which is often described as Paul's own interpretation of the eucharist.

This text contributes great depth to the meaning of participation. Participation in the eucharist consists of eating and drinking the sanctified bread and cup, which effects participation in the death of the Lord. To participate in the eucharist is to share in the Lord's self-giving in order to become self-giving oneself, and to build up a community whose being and life are governed by self-giving for the sake of the world. Paul is here criticizing the Corinthian church for its selfishness and self-indulgence at the expense of poorer members, precisely during the eucharistic celebration.

The Final Report of the Synod of 1985 says this:

> Liturgical reform cannot be restricted to ceremonies, rites, texts, etc.: active participation, so happily increased since the Council, consists not only in external activity, but first of all in interior and spiritual participation, a lively and fruitful sharing in the paschal Mystery of Christ (cf. SC 11).

Many liturgists would see here the truth of the axiom 'through the rite to the mystery'. A good summarizing text is found in GIRM 5:

> The celebration of the eucharist, and the entire liturgy, is carried out by the use of outward signs. By these signs faith is nourished, strengthened, and expressed. It is thus very important to select and arrange the forms and elements proposed by the Church, which, taking into account individual and local circumstances, will best foster active and full participation and promote the spiritual welfare of the faithful.

In conclusion, ritual participation in the liturgy is a participation in the mystery of salvation present in liturgical celebration; it is the right and duty of the community of the baptized.

Service and ministries

The same Holy Spirit who unites the assembly and makes it the celebrant of the liturgical celebration also endows it with a variety of ministries (see, e.g., 1 Corinthians 12:4–13; SC 26ff.).

That the whole assembly celebrates the liturgy is recognized by the post-Vatican II liturgical books and documents. This represents a shift in perception which needs to find expression in several ways. One of these is the way the celebrating space (the church building) is to be arranged (see GIRM 257). Another is the view that all the participants are, in principle, enabled to exercise the rich variety of ministries involved in worship. The celebration calls for as many ministries as the ritual needs.

Thus the role of the ordained priest is to be seen in terms of service of Christ–Church within the assembly. The theology and understanding of ordination today takes this into account, and the arrangement of the chapters of the major document of Vatican II, the Constitution on the Church, underlines it: chapter 1 deals with the Mystery of the Church as sacrament of trinitarian communion; chapter 2 deals with the People of God which is the Church as a body of believers who advance through history towards the fulfilment of all things. Not until chapter 3 is the ordained ministry dealt with.

The more Christians are imbued with the spirit of participation in the communion of God, Father, Son and Holy Spirit, the greater is their willingness to put themselves at the service of the community, in accordance with personal gifts and after due training, showing once again how the Church is a community of many gifts and one Spirit.

Authority, law, adaptation

These three associated areas are, in varying ways, of enormous importance for the Church. Certain fundamental principles may be mentioned here:

1. These elements of the visible Church are to be understood, exercised and carried out in the light of the theological nature of the liturgy. They are at the service of the promotion of the liturgy.
2. The laws of authority can seem external and remote. However, the more Christians enter into the mystery of the liturgy and are formed by its spirit, the more they will recognize that recent church teaching

and documents do in fact promote and consolidate the case for liturgical renewal. Lawmaking, at least in the liturgical sphere, is truly at the service of the work of salvation, present in the liturgical celebrations.

3. Liturgy is too important to be left entirely to local supervision and decision. The moderation of the liturgy needs the most competent people from the whole Church, who should act in close consultation with, and with full respect for, local communities with their insights and problems. This task is a service rather than an exercise of power.

4. The post-Vatican II liturgical books contain Introductions of a type quite distinct from the juridical and rubrical documents of earlier times. Though they contain directives and rules, they are grounded in rich theological, biblical, liturgical and spiritual presentations. Every attempt is made to offer a vision in the light of which the rules and directives can be understood.

5. It is increasingly recognized that rubrics and liturgical laws are of a very special nature because of their close relationship with the mystery of Christian worship, through which God reveals himself and his saving work. The laws of Christian celebration are derived from that sacred event; they protect it and express it.

Adaptation is dealt with by SC 37–40 and in other articles, and in further documents of the Council. There has followed a huge debate which shows no signs of coming to an end. In the light of what has been said, it will be clear that deep respect for the liturgical rites and texts is called for, since liturgical celebrations contain the presence of the Paschal Mystery of salvation, the free and unmerited gift of the grace of God. Their primary point of reference is the Paschal Mystery, and their most meaningful function is to reveal and signify that mystery. This they must be allowed to do without having inappropriate interpretations imposed on them.

However, rubrically correct celebration is not necessarily good celebration. Good celebration is that which allows the aims of the liturgy to be accomplished; it is done by people imbued with the spirit of the liturgy who look behind the rubrics to the reasons for them. Rubrics are guides and safeguards, not prison bars, and for the liturgical revolution set in motion by Vatican II to flourish, a thoughtful and generous approach is needed, not a narrow conformity. The Paschal Mystery is present not because of human rules but by God's great loving-kindness, which knows no bounds.

DOCUMENTATION AND BIBLIOGRAPHY

J. D. Crichton, *Christian Celebration: Understanding the Mass* (new edition; London: Geoffrey Chapman, 1992), chs 1, 2, 3 and 9.

John M. Huels, *Liturgical Law: An Introduction* (*American Essays in Liturgy* 4; Washington, DC: The Pastoral Press, 1987).

Frederick R. McManus, *Liturgical Participation: An Ongoing Assessment* (*American Essays in Liturgy* 10; Washington, DC: The Pastoral Press, 1988).

A. G. Martimort (ed.), *The Church at Prayer*, vol. I (London: Geoffrey Chapman, 1987).

D. A. Withey, *Catholic Worship: An Introduction to Liturgy* (Bury St Edmunds: Kevin Mayhew, 1990), ch. 8.

Unit 2

DEBORAH M. JONES

THE WORD OF GOD IN WORSHIP

Liturgical celebration is based primarily on the Word of God
(Lectionary for Mass, Introduction §3)
The treasures of the Bible are to be opened up more lavishly (SC
51)

The purpose of Scripture in worship

A useful insight is that of Paul VI in the Apostolic Constitution *Missale Romanum* (3 April 1969) prefaced to the Missal. Reflecting on the place of Scripture in liturgical celebration and on the Lectionary in particular, he writes: 'In accord with the teachings of the Second Vatican Council, all will thus regard sacred scripture as the abiding source of spiritual life, the foundation for Christian instruction, and the core of all theological study' (DOL 1362).

Any development of this theme should keep this vision at the forefront of its treatment of the Word of God:

- As an 'abiding source of spiritual life', the Word of God has to come to life in the experiences of individuals and communities. Hence the importance of hearing the Word, explaining it, meditating on it, and responding to it.
- As a 'foundation for Christian instruction', the Word of God must be at the centre of the theologizing of individuals and communities. The themes or propositions of the theology should arise out of Scripture rather than being imposed on the biblical text.
- As a 'core of all theological study', the Word of God must be approached in an adequate fashion taking into account the findings of contemporary biblical interpretation. This has tremendous implications for the preparation of readers, the direction of adult education programmes and, of course, for preaching.

Scripture recalls major events in our salvation history

Behind the words in our Bibles lie the experiences of a community convinced that through those historic experiences God's own self is revealed. The community expressed that conviction first in oral story, myth, legend and song. It then caused the writing, editing and collection of writings of that oral tradition in order to pass it on. We have inherited the sacred writings of our forerunners, both Jewish and Christian, in order to carry the tradition forward. They belong to the community and, inasmuch as we allow them to involve us, through them we recall our identity as a community, the body of Christ.

The occasion when we are most aware of our being community, the body of Christ, is in celebration, the liturgy. The supreme act of Catholic worship is the Mass, which is made up 'of the Liturgy of the Word and the Liturgy of the Eucharist, two parts so closely connected that they form but one single act of worship' (GIRM 28). Within this liturgy, the Word is heard afresh and God is revealed in a new, dynamic way, causing our hearts today 'to burn within us as he talked to us . . . and explained the scriptures to us' (Luke 24:32).

Call and response

The pattern of the operation of Scripture is one of call and response. The community is one which has been 'called out' by a God who chooses faithful people to be a 'light to the Gentiles' and a sign of God's own love.

- CALL. From the call to Abraham to set out in faith into the unknown, through the gathering of the disciples by Jesus, to the promises made for and by each baptized person, God calls each person by name to fulfil a task in this world which only that person can.

- RESPONSE. 'Speak, Lord, your servant is listening' (1 Samuel 3:10).

  - The Holy Spirit initiates all response to God, but we need to be open to his Word addressed to us. Only by investing the energy into active listening, can we begin to hear the Word.
  - The most natural way to respond to that which fills our heart is to do that for which we were made, to offer praise and worship.
  - From acknowledgement in awe and praise of our creator and saviour God, we naturally then desire to seek union with the source of our joy and hope, and so are led into communion in the sacraments enacted in the Church.

25

- Filled with the experience of God in word and sacrament, what else could we do but share this joy and hope with others? The obligation to mission is not optional, nor does commitment depend on feeling or fancy. 'They will not believe in [Jesus] unless they have heard of him, and they will not hear of him unless they get a preacher' (Romans 10:14–15). Preaching is not a function reserved to a few, the ordained for instance, but the task of all is to bring the word of God to our world of today.

Implications

'When the Scriptures are read in the church, it is Christ himself who is speaking' (SC 7). The way to acknowledge this presence of Christ in his Word is by creating an environment conducive to reverent, thoughtful worship.

Each symbol should speak clearly of the value which the community places on the Scriptures – the Book of the Gospels held high in dignified, ritual procession, with accompanying candles held at the same level and unrushed censing and kissing of the book. The Eastern rites include processions among the congregation, enabling worshippers to touch the sacred pages with kissed fingers with which they then cross themselves.

Each material element needs to reflect the best which the culture offers. The ambo, from which the Word is read, the lectionary and Book of the Gospels, the candles themselves, should be of fine quality, and pleasing appearance, and in keeping with the scale and style of the building.

The attitude of all taking part is one of attentiveness. 'Listen, Israel ... Let the words I urge on you today be written on your heart' (Deuteronomy 24:4, 6).

The approach to the ambo and pulpit will be purposeful and reverent. Unnecessary words, like numbering the readings or announcing: 'The responsorial psalm, and the response is ...' or 'sit ... stand ...', should be omitted. Moments of reflective silence should be maintained between reading and psalm, and reading and acclamation. Clear acknowledgements that 'This is the word, or the Gospel, of the Lord' should be made, eliciting the enthusiastic response 'Thanks be to God' and a full-hearted 'Praise to you, Lord Jesus Christ'.

'All taking part' means, of course, the whole worshipping community, not just the ones 'up front'. The community has the right to hear the Word proclaimed in the most effective way possible. People should not feel left out because they cannot hear or do not follow what is going on.

Provision should be made for various groups:

- people with hearing difficulties (installing a 'loop' system, and signing can help);
- children who need to experience their own specially adapted Liturgy of the Word;
- catechumens and those who cannot be presupposed to have heard the basic proclamation of the Gospel;
- noisy babies and tots who need to be looked after to enable others to hear and to create silences when appropriate.

Preaching

> The homily, an integral part of the liturgy of the word, is a continuation of God's saving message which elicits faith and conversion. It is neither exegesis nor moral exhortation but a joyful proclamation of God's saving deeds in Christ. Basing his preaching on the liturgical texts, the homilist breaks the bread of God's Word by actualizing it, by showing how God is continuing to act and speak among his people today. Through the homily the members of the assembly are called to become a holy people so that they can better celebrate the eucharist and offer themselves with and through Christ in the eucharistic prayer. (US Bishops' Conference, *Study Guide for the Order of Mass*)

Elements of the Liturgy of the Word

Structure of the Liturgy of the Word

> Readings from scripture are the heart of the Liturgy of the Word. The homily, responsorial psalms, profession of faith, and general intercessions develop and complete it. In the readings God speaks to his people and nourishes their spirit; Christ is present through his Word. The homily explains the readings. The chants and the profession of faith comprise the people's acceptance of God's word. It is of primary importance that the people hear God's message of love, digest it with the aid of psalms, silence, and the homily, and respond, involving themselves in the great covenant of love and redemption. All else is secondary. (US Catholic Conference, *Music in Catholic Worship* 45)

All of the above should be included in every liturgy. In many parts of the world, the Catholic faith is regularly nourished and celebrated by liturgies of the Word alone, with no eucharistic liturgies for weeks, months or even years.

The structure of the Liturgy of the Word has its roots in pre-Christian Jewish synagogue worship. There each week a lengthy extract (*sidra*, divided into seven sections or *parashah*) is read from the Torah (Genesis, Exodus, Leviticus, Numbers, Deuteronomy). The Torah reading is accompanied by an appropriate reading (*haftarah*) from one of the books of the Prophets. The whole Torah is read over a three-year cycle. Before and after each reading God is blessed for providing his Word, and the scroll is processed between its resting place in an Ark, or decorated cupboard, and the Bimah, or reading desk.

There would then follow a homily. In the Acts of the Apostles, we can see that St Paul and his companions in Antioch

> went to the synagogue on the sabbath and took their seats.
> After the lessons (readings) of the Law (Torah) and the Prophets
> had been read, the presidents of the synagogue sent them a
> message: 'Brothers, if you would like to address some words
> of encouragement to the congregation, please do so'. Paul stood
> up, held up a hand for silence and began to speak ... As they
> left they were asked to preach on the same theme the following
> sabbath ... (Acts 13:14b–16, 42)

For an example of Our Lord's preaching where he uses one text from the Torah and another text from the Prophets, read John 6, noting verses 31 (from Exodus 16:4) and 45 (Isaiah 54:13).

In the synagogue, as in church, prayers are made on behalf of others, especially public authorities, religious leaders and communities, and for people in need. Frequent psalms, chosen for their liturgical appropriateness, are sung during the seder, or service.

When Church and synagogue eventually split, Jewish Christians continued many of the practices familiar to them, adapting and reinterpreting them as the Church has done with all its customs throughout the ages. The gospel replaces the Torah reading, and an Old Testament reading replaces one specifically from the Prophets (although the books of the prophets in the Hebrew Bible include the 'historical' books: Joshua, Samuel, Kings and Judges).

With the disposition of readings – Old Testament (read) – psalm (sung) – New Testament (read) – acclamation (sung) – gospel (read) – (frequently followed by a sung acclamation) – there should be no effect of simply piling words on words. Sung elements really must be sung. The psalm was composed to be sung or chanted, never read through like prose. The acclamation (omitted if there is only one reading plus a psalm before the gospel) is intended to provide musical accompaniment during the procession to the ambo of the reader of the gospel, the Book of the Gospels and attendant candle-bearers and censers.

Even the readings themselves could occasionally be chanted – for example, the gospel of Easter Sunday. Chanting is the hallowed means of proclaiming scriptures in many traditions, including our own until recently. Nowadays it is likely to be something exceptional, but music could perhaps occasionally be played softly *underneath* some readings. Song, chant and Word proclaimed and silently meditated upon together create an aesthetic liturgical experience of harmonious variety and interest. Choir, cantors, instrumentalists and readers all have to be ready to link their sections with the others in a smooth and seamless rhythm. Readers particularly should plan their journey to the ambo to ensure no undue delay, which can cause worries to set in over what happens next!

The homily

The Word then leads us more deeply into the mystery of the living God through the gentle guidance of the homilist. The homilist lets 'the bread of the Word be truly shared as "nourishment for the Christian life" ' (GIRM 41).

All the baptized are called to be homilists, to interpret the Good News to the world around us using today's language and with images as fresh and lively as were those of Jesus in first-century Palestine. The homily encourages all of us to engage in Scripture's process – that of reflecting on experiences in our lives, individually and collectively, and seeing in them God's activity and purposes.

Two terms in the languages of the Bible give an insight into the function of the homily. The Hebrew equivalent, *midrash*, means 'enquiry', interpretation which seeks to go below the surface of the text to arrive at its spirit, using a range of examples in the form of legends, parables and moral teachings which illustrate the kernel of meaning behind the text.

The word 'homily' comes from the Greek *homilein* which literally means 'to converse familiarly with'. Maybe the conversing in Corinth became too much for Paul to take, with the Corinthian women chipping in and interrupting, so that he asked them to wait till they got home to discuss the homily! (1 Corinthians 14:34, 35).

Jean Lebon (*How to Understand the Liturgy*, London: SCM, 1987) lists eight ways in which the homily can fulfil its function (useful technical terms are given in parenthesis):

1. By explaining the reading, providing its context and author's meaning (exegesis)
2. By making it relevant so that 'today this word is fulfilled' (Luke 4:21)
3. By proclaiming the paschal mystery of which every word is an integral part (kerygma)
4. By teaching every aspect of the history of salvation (catechesis)
5. By explaining the meaning of the sacramental signs (mystagogia)
6. By helping us to discern signs of the Kingdom of God now (prophecy)
7. By giving witness, through using examples of people's personal testimony
8. By exhorting and encouraging.

Not, of course, that all these aspects can be covered every time.

Whether the homily begins with the text (known as the 'from above' approach) or with a situation from life (the 'from below' approach), it must be based on the Scripture of the readings, directed to the real concerns of the people assembled, and taken up in worship. Preparation and delivery will take note not only of contemporary scholarship but also of the culture of the people, which in the West has 'passed beyond the civilisation of the word ... Today (people live) in the civilisation of the image' (*Evangelii Nuntiandi* 42). It is the imagination of people today, fed by a rapid succession of thirty-second TV ad 'stories', which needs to be challenged and inspired. David Tracy (*Blessed Rage for Order*, New York: Seabury Press, 1975) urges homilists to move towards a non-conceptualist approach closer to that of Jesus himself: 'Human beings need story, symbol, image, myth, and fiction to disclose to their imaginations some genuinely new possibilities for existence; possibilities which conceptual analysis, committed as it is to understanding present actualities, cannot adequately provide ... Fictions open our minds, our imaginations and our hearts.'

How is the homilist to know how (or even if) the homily has been received? There is no communication where there is no reception or response, so some method for evaluation needs to be arranged, more than the vague awareness of attention or the polite nod at the church door. A representative section of the community might meet with the homilist once a week or twice a month, both to help prepare the next homily and to comment constructively on the previous one.

The profession of faith

Inspired by the Word of God proclaimed and broken for them, the people then express their faith in the creed. This is not a prayer but a public affirmation of faith, to be recited in unison at such a volume that passers-by should be able to hear. This is our collective testimony to the world, not a mumbled recollection of private faith.

The creed, formerly a baptismal element, was introduced into the Sunday liturgy just before the Lord's Prayer by some parts of the Church at the end of the sixth century, to ensure the orthodoxy of large numbers of converts from such prevailing heresies as Arianism. Charlemagne, around 800, moved it to just after the gospel (and, incidentally, insisted on the 'and the Son' (*Filioque*) clause over which Orthodox and Catholic have been in dispute ever since). However, it was not until the twelfth century that the creed became universal, Rome being the last place to introduce it into the Mass.

Because much of the creed is duplicated in the following Eucharistic Prayer, and it is a repetitive response to theological problems which are not of immediate concern today, there is some justification in a call for the Church to provide an alternative creed for the contemporary world.

The General Instruction on the Roman Missal (GIRM) enjoins everyone to bow their heads at the words 'by the power of the Holy Spirit' (98).

Intercessions

GIRM: 'The people, exercising their priestly function, intercede for all humanity ... the whole assembly gives expression to its supplication either by a response said together after each Intention, or by silent prayer' (45). Just as the synagogue worship includes formal prayers of Intercession (see above), so did the early Church. By the middle of the second century, Justin Martyr (*First Apology* 65) reports that the first act of the newly baptized is to stay in church for the common prayers of the faithful. Previously, as catechumens, they would have left before or after the gospel. Recited standing, the prayers were concluded with a kiss of peace. The Solemn Prayers of Good Friday probably resemble most closely the form of these intercessions in the West:

> The priest calls on, or bids, the people to pray for X.
> The deacon then directs the people to kneel for silent prayer.
> After a few moments he calls them to rise.
> The priest then draws together (collects) the prayers in a
> Collect.

The Church in the East made the intercessions in the form of a litany, brief biddings sung by a deacon, with the people repsonding to each with 'Kyrie eleison', concluded by a collect from the priest. In the West, Pope Gelasius (492–496) adopted the Eastern Kyrie litany and inserted it just before the readings. The intercessions *after* the readings then fell out of use until their restoration by Vatican II and the Kyrie litany lost its invocations, although something similar has been restored in Penitential Rite III. The Gloria after the Kyrie was introduced for every Sunday and feast day Mass in the eleventh century as part of the preparation rites.

The restored bidding prayer, also known as 'General Intercessions' and 'Prayers of the Faithful', should be composed and led by the faithful. Possibly a different group or organization within the parish could take responsibility each week for composing them. Prayers composed far in advance, or taken from books, can surely not reflect the needs which arise and are on people's minds at the time of the liturgy. To ignore the wars, famines and disasters which fill the TV screens, and local concerns in the neighbourhood, is to give the impression that the Church is out of touch with the world and to leave compassionate people frustrated.

Prayers of Intercession should follow the sequence:

(a) for the needs of the Church
(b) for public authorities and the salvation of the world
(c) for those oppressed by any need
(d) for the local community.

It must be remembered that these are *requests for prayer*, not the prayers themselves which are made silently by the people. The requests should be brief and simply phrased, not introduced with 'Lord, we pray that ...' or 'Dear Jesus, help ...'. It is not necessary to furnish all possible details of the subject for prayer, nor is it helpful to be so unfocused that there are no actual, imaginable subjects for whom the people are to pray.

Also it is essential to remember to give time for silent prayer. Maybe a count to ten after each bidding would help.

The concluding Marian prayer with which we are familiar in England and Wales is in fact unique to these countries, and its introduction in the early 1970s did not greatly please the Roman authorities.

Preparation

1. Spiritual

Like all liturgy, the Liturgy of the Word is a public, community activity. It is not designed to be a time for private reading from missals and missalettes. If people have to resort to individually isolating reading, that could be saying something about the quality of proclamation. Attentive, active listening should help us to experience God's word for us – challenging, transforming, inspiring, consoling.

To gain most benefit, time should be spent in advance preparing for reception of the Word proclaimed, not only by God's mouthpiece (*nebi* in Hebrew = prophet) the reader, but by all.

Prepare – by careful reading of the texts, several times, praying that God's Spirit will enlighten your mind and touch your heart by the message of his Word.

Prepare – by looking up the texts in the Bible (preferably in the same version, the Jerusalem Bible, as in the Lectionary).
Read around the text, ignoring chapter and verse division (devices invented relatively recently: chapters by Stephen Langton, Archbishop of Canterbury, in 1226, and verses by a French printer, Robert Estienne, in 1551).

Prepare – by looking up obscure words and references in a good concordance or commentary (of which *The New Jerome Biblical Commentary* is probably the best).

If at all possible, prepare in groups, and take every opportunity of following courses in Scripture study and in biblical faith-sharing.

> To ignore Scripture is to ignore Christ. (Pope Benedict XV, after St Jerome)

Biblical

To achieve an understanding of how the Bible fits together repays all efforts. Confusion and bewilderment, particularly over Old Testament readings ('Did God really want all those people killed?'), can be dispelled with a grasp of the development of theology and the variety of source traditions. From the Torah/Pentateuch, through the Prophets and the Writings (including the Deuterocanonical books), to the New Testament, the basic message of God's faithful, saving love and compassion to all creatures, despite all the horrors of human sinfulness and limitation, can be seen in a multitude of different forms and expressions. The meaning of the Bible for today, for each of us, needs the support of knowing as much as we can about the meaning it had when it was written, who wrote it, when and why, and what it meant to those who determined the canon of Scripture and the generations of believers, both Jewish and Christian, through whom it has been passed down.

Liturgical

The selection of biblical texts for the Lectionary was determined by their liturgical use. The Sunday Lectionary in use since 1969 differs from its predecessor in many ways. Before, only two readings, both from the New Testament, were offered each week and the same readings occurred every year.

Then the bishops at Vatican II urged that 'a more representative portion of the scriptures be read to the people over a set cycle of years' and that the Word of God should be opened up 'more lavishly, so that richer fare may be provided for the faithful'.

Now the Word is proclaimed over a cycle of three years. The gospels take priority, controlling the theme and choice of the Old Testament reading. Each year of the cycle is characterized by one of the three synoptic gospels, although the highlight of the Church's year, the Paschal Mystery (Lent–Easter season) makes use of the gospel of John, accompanied appropriately by that record of the first Easter people, the Acts of the Apostles.

The Advent–Christmas season differs by being 'theme'-led, with each of the three readings following a single theme, with the pattern as follows:

First Sunday: Messiah's Second Coming in glory at the end of time
Second and Third Sundays: John the Baptist announces the coming
      of Messiah
Fourth Sunday: Messiah is about to be born

Every Sunday a response of praise follows the first reading, drawn from the treasury of songs for Israel's Temple liturgy. This psalm should be sung by cantor or choir, with a refrain taken up by the people. There is nothing wrong with varying this formula to keep alive the freshness and enthusiasm of this act of worship. Some psalms suggest appropriate actions to accompany them.

The second reading, other than in the Advent–Christmas and Lent seasons, has no 'tie-in' with the Old Testament/gospel theme, being taken from the letters of the New Testament Church. One difficulty with understanding extracts out of their context is that no allowance is made for changes and developments in the writers and their recipients from one letter to another.

2. Technical

(The following applies to all who proclaim the Word as readers.)

Reading skills

Most people in the West can read quietly to themselves. Few people, however, can read aloud effectively in public without some training. This is just a fact – it implies no shame or stigma, although the reluctance of some readers to receive advice from others can produce some lacklustre and unfortunate performances. Readers could minister to each other by passing honest comment on the quality of proclamation each week. Regular group practice, taking turns to read and facing up to constructive criticism, would help to pull up standards in this crucial ministry.

The qualities which are tested by the English Speaking Board (International) in their adjudications of oral skills are:

- Comprehension, communication and clarity
- Sense, sensibility and sincerity
- Rapport, response and reception.

Their advice would include

- thorough preparation, when possible, of the text involved;
- scan the whole sentence before speaking;
- propel the opening phrase, looking up from the text;
- speak slowly and clearly, attending to the nuances of punctuation and key words;
- ensure the voice does not drop or tail off at the end of sentences, and that final consonants are clearly marked (e.g. 'Lor' could be Lord or Law);
- make sure that what you have said has been *received*.

Above all, and beyond technical perfection, the infectiousness of faith, the enthusiasm of a reader in love with God, God's Word and God's people, will be communicated with the help of the Holy Spirit.

Mechanical aids

Highly effective training can be achieved by the use of a camcorder (video camera) and playback television receiver. Let each reader be filmed then play back the performance for group criticism. It is much easier, and less embarrassing, to comment on a recorded performance than on the memory of a live one. The readers themselves can see and hear as others do, and learn many valuable lessons. An audio recorder can play a similar, if less effective, role.

Wherever a microphone is used, it is highly desirable to practise the technique required to be heard distinctly, without boom and distortion. Attention needs to be paid to the distance required between mouth and microphone, how to adjust the height and direction to suit and what volume is necessary to project the sound. If the microphone does not seem to be working and has no on/off switch, avoid tapping or blowing onto it, just breathe more deeply and project your natural voice to the back of the roof.

In every congregation there are probably several people with hearing difficulties who use hearing aids. The use of a 'loop' system, which helps to amplify target sounds and eliminate some of the background interference, can make all the difference. As well as major systems which can be installed unobtrusively along the pews of churches, there are also available portable systems for smaller spaces. These consist of a box the size of a couple of books, a clip-on microphone and a length of flex which can be placed in a circle around the room or part of the room.

Another consideration can be the adaptation of facilities to enable a wheelchair-using person to exercise the ministry of reader, and/or the provision of a Braille lectionary or text for a blind reader.

Gesture and posture

At the lectern, see that the Lectionary is at the right height for comfort, wait for people to be ready and, during the reading, make frequent eye-contact. As well as helping to engage the attention of the listeners, this also ensures that you face frontwards and not downwards, masking the voice. Use your finger, if you need to, on the margin of the Lectionary to mark your place.

After the readings, bow your head and, with eyes closed, mark 20–30 seconds' silence for people to begin to digest the Word. Similarly, pause for the count of ten after each 'Bidding Prayer' before leading the invocation of the Lord to hear. It is in this pause that the people pray as they have been bidden.

Movement

It is better for readers to emerge from among the congregation, than to lurk behind pillars in the sanctuary or seem to add to the clerical caste. An exception can be made for the first reader if he/she has been included in the Entrance Procession.

All movements should be made with dignity but without obsequiousness, and all fluster and rush should be strenuously avoided. It is worth rehearsing the procedure for approaching and leaving the ambo, checking if there are any steps or obstacles to negotiate and if there is any way of controlling the height of the lectern.

Always check the Lectionary before the liturgy to see where the readings are on the page and that the correct page is open or marked with ribbon.

DOCUMENTATION AND BIBLIOGRAPHY

Constitution on the Liturgy, 24, 35–36, 51–52.

Second Vatican Council, Dogmatic Constitution on Divine Revelation, *Dei Verbum*; included in Austin Flannery (ed.) *Documents of the Second Vatican Council* (Dublin: Dominican Publications, 1975/Leominster: Fowler Wright Books, 1981).

General Instruction on the Roman Missal, 8, 9, 33–47.

Lectionary for Mass: Introduction; included in Flannery.

Lawrence J. Johnson, *The Word and Eucharist Handbook* (San Jose, CA: Resource Publications, 1986).

Ralph A. Keifer, *To Hear and Proclaim* (Washington, DC: The Pastoral Press): a commentary on the Introduction to the Lectionary for Mass.

D. A. Withey, *Catholic Worship* (Bury St Edmunds: Kevin Mayhew, 1990), ch. 10.

ALAN GRIFFITHS

THE EUCHARIST

> At the Last Supper Christ instituted the sacrifice and Paschal
> Meal that makes the sacrifice of the cross continually present in
> the church when the priest, representing the Lord, carries out
> what the Lord did and handed over to his disciples to do in his
> memory.
>
> Christ took the bread and cup and gave the cup; he broke the
> bread and gave it to his disciples, saying: 'Take and eat, this is my
> body.' Giving the cup he said 'Take and drink, this is the cup of
> my blood. Do this in memory of me.' (GIRM 48)

'Eucharist'

In this section we look briefly at Jesus's own background of prayer
and worship and at what he said and did in the Last Supper. We look
at how these things have become, over hundreds of years, the ritual
that we now call the Mass or the eucharist.

Eucharist is a Greek word. It means thanksgiving. 'Thanksgiving' is
an essential feature of Jewish prayer. Since Jesus and his disciples were
Jews, this Jewish background to Christian liturgy needs to be understood in order to grasp some of the basic ideas of Christian liturgical
activity. So it is appropriate to begin this section with some remarks
on Jewish prayer and worship.

Blessing and giving thanks

People frequently ask priests to bless things. If we use words, these
are likely to be words of 'invocation', the equivalent of 'God, please
bless this . . .'.

It is as if we are asking God to take the object over. The implication
is that the object does not already belong to God's creation, or that it
needs some 'religious' sanction before being used for a devout purpose.

If you had asked Jesus, or any of his contemporaries in Palestine to
bless an object, they might at first not have understood exactly what
you were wanting. But if they obliged you, they would not have asked

38

God to bless the object in question. They would have *blessed God for that object*, for its very existence as a gift of God.

The blessing of lighted candles on the eve of the Jewish Sabbath is a good example. The woman of the house lights the candles on the supper table and recites the following blessing: 'Blessed are you, Lord, Master of the universe, you make us holy by your laws and command us to kindle the Sabbath light.' This is not a blessing *of* the light but a blessing of God *for* the light. The light is God's gift.

A further feature of this form of blessing is that it recounts a work of God: 'You have made us holy by your laws ...'. The tradition of blessing involves a naming of God's works. Other Jewish blessings involve more extended thanksgivings – records of God's great deeds for the salvation of his people.

The blessing of God together with praise and thanksgiving is the predominant feature of Jewish prayer. It is an unbroken tradition. It is the tradition of Jesus of Nazareth. So, via our Lord and the apostles, it has become Christian tradition. The greatest of our prayers begins with this: 'Lift up your hearts ... Let us give thanks to the Lord our God.'

There is another assumption at work in Jewish prayer and celebration. When the deeds of God are proclaimed, they are still vital to us now; we are being brought close to them. God never revokes the wonderful works that he has performed. The Jewish Passover celebration, for example, has the rubric that each one who celebrates the Passover meal must think of themselves as present at the Exodus from Egypt, for it was not just for the ancestors that God did these wonderful things. It was 'for us as well', Jews of whatever time or place.

For a Jew, to perform a ritual act in remembrance of an event was for performer and event to be somehow made contemporary. It is this understanding that makes the Jewish and Christian concept of 'remembrance' or 'memorial' so full of meaning for our liturgy. When we meet to celebrate Mass, it is within this tradition. The words 'in memory of me' mean much more than 'to remember me'. It is difficult to put the meaning of that into words. The 'memory' or 'memorial act' of Jesus means the *presence* of Jesus; all he was, all he is, all he is to be.

Passover

Passover, the spring feast of Exodus and unleavened bread, was the time of Jesus' crucifixion. His 'Passover' into the radiant light of resurrection is the new Christian sense of Passover. We still keep this Jewish feast. In Greek and Latin 'Easter' is *Pascha*, the Hebrew rendered into

Greek. From this we get 'Paschal' as in candle, vigil, Paschal time and so on. We celebrate a Christian Passover, we have kept up this ancient feast with all its new, Christ-centred meaning. St Paul says: 'Christ, our Passover, is sacrificed. Let us keep the feast with the unleavened bread of sincerity and truth' (1 Corinthians 5:7–8). The ancient Roman Eucharistic Prayer for the Paschal Vigil uses this Jewish imagery: 'Christ has become our Paschal sacrifice. He is the true Lamb who took away the sins of the world.'

For Jews, the sense of being close to the foundation events of Exodus, Sinai, covenant is, perhaps more than anywhere, heightened at Passover. So for Christians, our eucharist contains that same closeness to the event that brought us salvation, the Paschal Mystery of our Lord Jesus Christ.

The New Testament: the Last Supper

The Last Supper was a Jewish meal, much like the meals Jesus held on all sabbaths and festivals. The Last Supper was eaten at Passover time. Matthew, Mark and Luke agree that it was *the* Passover meal. John seems to say that the Last Supper took place twenty-four hours before Passover proper began. For our purposes this is not of the first importance. Jewish ritual meals had a basically similar structure. We might think of it as 'grace before meal', 'meal' and 'grace after meal'. These graces, like all Jewish ritual prayers, took the form of blessings and thanksgiving. They were done with bread before the meal and a special cup of wine at the end of the meal.

At the Last Supper Jesus blessed God for the bread, then broke and distributed it. 'This is my body', he said. After the meal Jesus blessed and thanked God for wine and also for the Law, the Promised Land, all God's gifts. He probably also prayed for God's continuing mercy upon his people. He passed the cup among his disciples. 'This is the cup of my blood.'

The tradition of the Church takes up these actions of Jesus because they give the structure or ritual shape to our eucharist. This is a simple shape. It consists of:

(a) prayer of blessing and thanksgiving and supplication
(b) breaking the bread and sharing the bread and cup.

The actions of Jesus give the structure to our eucharist; the words of Jesus give the meaning to our eucharist. Somehow Jesus was identifying himself, his whole self ('body' and 'blood' are code words for the wholeness of his presence) with the actions he was performing in the company of his disciples. So for Christians, eucharist has always meant more than just a reminder or flashback to the Last Supper.

It is not unreasonable to suppose that Jesus and his disciples celebrated regular meal rituals. As observant Jews they could not do otherwise. So the Last Supper cannot be regarded historically as the sole source of the eucharistic ritual. It is better to say that eucharist is a Jewish meal ritual endowed with new meaning by Christ and the Church. The ritual of the Last Supper provided the ritual of the eucharist. Jesus, the crucified and risen one, is the meaning of that ritual, wholly present under the appearances of bread and wine.

The eucharistic structure is used by the gospels in other places, probably on purpose. For example, if you look at the feeding miracles (John 6) or the Emmaus narrative in Luke 24, you will find the same structure. To put this structure in chart form would look like this:

'He took the bread'
'He said the blessing'
'He broke the bread'
'He gave it to his disciples and said . . .'
THE MEAL WAS EATEN

After the meal:

'He took the cup'
'Again he gave you thanks and praise'
'He gave the cup to his disciples and said . . .'

With that series of seven actions built round a meal, Jesus gave us the eucharist.

The eucharist in the early Church

The eucharistic ritual that has been listed above underwent two important changes in the course of its passage out of the New Testament and into the history of the Christian Church. We can follow these changes if we go to the first Christian witness to the full celebration of the eucharist, Justin Martyr, who was writing about AD 150.

Born in Samaria, Justin was converted to Christianity about AD 130. He wrote two books: *Dialogue with Trypho* and later the *Apology*. It is in this second work that Justin gives us the outline of the principal Christian Sunday service, in which it is possible for us to recognize our Sunday eucharist. This is the outline that he gives:

Readings from the apostles or the prophets

Discourse on the reading by the presiding minister
Prayers of intercession
The sign of peace
Presentation of bread and wine
Prayer of praise and thanksgiving by the presiding minister to which
    everyone present replies 'Amen'
Distribution of the bread and wine by the deacons.

Clearly this structure is basic to our Sunday Mass. Indeed, everything
that has happened since the middle of the second century is but an
elaboration of this basic structure, not a fundamental change in it.
However, when we compare this structure with what we saw in the
New Testament, we notice developments.

1. The Jewish structure is a ritual meal. At an early date, the Christians
   removed the meal (or reordered the structure to eat the meal later)
   and combined the two ritual blessings of bread and cup into one
   long prayer. We call this prayer the *Eucharistic Prayer*.

   The Eucharistic Prayer begins with the ancient dialogue (probably
   the oldest words in our liturgy) 'Lift up your hearts', 'Let us give
   thanks to the Lord our God' and proceeds via the acclamation 'Holy,
   holy' to the final 'Through him, with him, in him', or doxology. This
   Eucharistic Prayer is the *essential* spoken part of the Mass.
   The early Christians kept the breaking of bread, a necessary gesture
   for distribution as well as a profound symbolic action, then shared the
   eucharistic bread and cup. In this way, by the time of Justin the Church
   had already 'arranged' the actions of Jesus to give the shape of our
   eucharistic liturgy.

2. Justin shows us this liturgy augmented by a 'liturgy of the Word'
   with homily and prayer of intercession. This (presumably) is part of
   the Church's inheritance from the synagogue and was at an early
   date attached to the Liturgy of the Eucharist.

   So the two major changes that had already taken place by the time
   of Justin were firstly the emergence of the Liturgy of the Word as
   the usual companion to eucharist, and secondly the structure of the
   eucharist itself, in the removal of the meal element and the rearrangement of the New Testament scheme.
   To make this completely clear, here is a comparative chart showing
   all the differences between the liturgy that the disciples inherited from
   their Jewish tradition and from Jesus and the full liturgical shape given
   150 years later by Justin.

Last Supper

Justin

Thursday (probably)
evening
within a meal
unrelated to synagogue
annual celebration
seven-action shape

Sunday
daybreak
no meal
Liturgy of the Word
weekly celebration
four-action shape

Seven-action shape

Four-action shape

taking bread, taking wine
blessing bread, wine
breaking
distribution of bread then wine

taking both together
blessing both together
breaking
distribution of both together

Summary of developing shape:

Stage 1: bread – meal – cup
Stage 2: meal – bread and cup
Stage 3: Liturgy of the Word – Liturgy of the bread and cup

The Second Vatican Council

The Constitution on the Sacred Liturgy (SC) was the first of the documents promulgated by the Second Vatican Council. Chapter 1 of this handbook has already explained the general principles governing revision and reform of the Roman liturgy. The Constitution summarized the understanding of the liturgy that the Council was laying down and set up the machinery that was necessary for a comprehensive reform of the Roman Rite.

Specifically, SC 47–58 relate to the eucharist. These paragraphs should be read before studying what follows.

The Constitution says that liturgy is an act of the whole Church. All Christ's faithful people must take their rightful part in it. This is 'participation'. It is rooted in the Council's understanding of the Church's nature and deepest reality. Liturgical participation expresses in tangible form that all Christ's people are involved in the mystery of salvation which is the mystery of Christ. Liturgy, like the mystery of salvation, is in the first person plural.

SC 49–58 give specific directions for reform of the order of Mass, and deal with three important questions:

1. Ritual and meanings
2. The availability of Scripture

3. Liturgical language.

The Council took its lead from the liturgical movement and taught that active participation in the liturgy should be the aim of the whole process of reform. The Constitution concludes that all elements of liturgy, whether action or word, should be accessible to those who participate.

Ritual meaning

The ritual of the eucharist had inevitably got more elaborate as the centuries passed. Rites developed in response to historical, cultural and theological developments. The Council wanted rites to be simplified, not to lose their accumulated meanings but to let these meanings speak more clearly. Specifically, four elements were mentioned:

1. The homily was to be restored. A homily is not a sermon. A sermon is a 'set piece' independent of any liturgical context. A homily exists as part of the Mass and should therefore be drawn from the Mass, from the reading of Scripture or other texts of the Mass being celebrated.
2. The prayer of the faithful was also to be restored to the Mass as the Church's universal prayer for the needs of all creation. In response to the Word of God the Church exercises a priestly ministry of intercession. The Consilium (the body responsible for implementing the reform agenda) produced a document on the prayer of the faithful in 1965.
3. Communion. The Constitution made provision for communion from the chalice on certain occasions: at ordinations, religious profession and marriages, to those ordained or professed or married. These were given as examples. The directive left the way open for the Holy See and local bishops to broaden the provision, as has progressively been done.

   The Council reasserted the traditional (and 'more complete form of participation') rule for Holy Communion. Communion was to be given from the bread consecrated at the Mass being celebrated. Communion should not be given from the tabernacle.
4. Language. The Liturgy Constitution began the process by which the Mass was eventually to be celebrated in the vernacular. The various instructions that followed the release of the Liturgy Constitution amplified this process. In the first instance, the readings and the General Intercessions and (optionally) the 'people's parts' (unspecified) were also to be in the vernacular.
5. The opening up of sacred Scripture. The lectionary contained in the

old Roman Missal was a one-year lectionary giving two readings for all but a few Masses. Readings, especially those for Sundays, were usually from the New Testament. The Old Testament was little represented. This lectionary was not constructed in any systematic fashion (though early in its history it may have been), and was poorly representative of the Bible as a whole.

The Council desired that the Word of God should be accessible to God's people since the Church is formed and animated by the Word of God. The Constitution asked for a greater use of scriptural texts in the Mass, more systematically arranged over a longer period of time than had been the case hitherto. This opened the way to the new Lectionary with its three-year cycle of Scripture readings.

The machinery for reform

Pope Paul VI, by his Motu Proprio *Sacram Liturgiam* of 1964, set up machinery for reform and orientated the Consilium which was to oversee the whole process. One or two provisions were also made with immediate effect, with respect to setting up of Liturgy Commissions in dioceses, the celebration of confirmation and matrimony within the Mass, and the use of the vernacular in the Divine Office.

The Sacred Congregation of Rites and later the Congregation of Divine Worship produced three 'Instructions' over the next six years, in 1964, 1967 and 1970. It is essential to read these instructions to see the progress of the reform up as far as the appearance of the revised Roman Missal in 1969.

The first instruction of September 1964, known by its Latin title of *Inter Oecumenici*, made provision for the liturgical formation of those training for ordained ministry and members of religious institutes. It gave some guidance in the question of 'competent authority', i.e. who can initiate liturgical reforms. It laid down guidelines for the simplification of existing rites, norms for the translation of texts and for musical compositions, made provisional reforms in the Order of Mass and further specified the occasions when the vernacular might be used.

The second instruction known by its Latin opening as *Tres Abhinc Annos* appeared in 1967. This document contained further modifications of rubrics and provision for further simplification of Mass rites in expectation of the appearance of the new Roman Missal.

The third instruction, *Liturgicae Instaurationes*, appeared in 1970 after the appearance of the new Roman Missal. Its tone was therefore different from that of the preceding instructions. It reasserted the principles underlying the new rites and clarified issues arising from them. It was more like a short set of guidelines for the use of the Roman Missal.

The Roman Missal of 1970

On 3 April 1969, by the Apostolic Constitution *Missale Romanum*, Pope Paul VI launched the Roman Missal revised according to the decrees of the Second Vatican Council. This was the first thorough reform of the Missal for 400 years, but not the first reform altogether. Since 1570, successive editions of the Roman Missal kept pace with new texts for feasts and votive masses and, after 1950, with the extensive revisions of the Liturgy of Holy Week. The most recent of the new editions was that promulgated in 1962. Revision and reform were no strangers to the Roman Missal.

The Council of Trent, in its concern to create an understanding and committed body of Catholic faithful, had stressed, in addition to the unitary nature of the Roman liturgy, the value of the Mass in strengthening understanding of the mystery of faith. A similar concern is voiced in the apostolic constitution of Paul VI. The new Missal was pronounced to be, as part of the heritage of the Council of Trent as well as Vatican II, 'a witness to unchanging tradition'.

However, the Apostolic Constitution was not quite frank about its desire to improve on some of the Tridentine legislation. For example, on communion under both kinds, it admitted to a re-evaluation of the Tridentine provisions, hindered as those had been by the extreme views of the Reformed Churches on the subject of communion from the chalice.

The liturgical movement had made this whole reform more or less a certainty when its tenets received official approval from Pius XII in 1947 in the encyclical letter *Mediator Dei*. It was the Council however that provided the necessary stimulus to begin in earnest the complete work of revision.

The new Roman Missal was prefaced by a lengthy introduction known as the General Instruction on the Roman Missal. This document expands upon the contents of the Apostolic Constitution, spelling out the developments that had, since 1570 and most particularly since 1903, made a reform of the liturgy necessary. Principally, the General Instruction lists the themes that the liturgical movement had introduced into the thinking of the pre-conciliar Church.

1. The eucharist is a 'mystery' which carries out the work of our redemption each time it is celebrated.
2. The eucharist is the exercise of the priestly office of the whole Church (including, of course, the ordained ministry).

3. The eucharist is a place of teaching that needs to be accessible to the faithful, in particular through use of the vernacular.

The Order of the Mass

The celebration of Mass brings to us in and through the Church all that God has done in Christ for the salvation of humankind. In the celebration of Mass, through the Church, we take up as our prayer and sacrifice the prayer and work of Christ which culminated in the Paschal Mystery of his death and resurrection. That active engagement in the mystery of salvation is outwardly or sacramentally expressed by active participation in the celebration of the eucharist. The invitation of Jesus is to 'do this in memory of me'.

We participate essentially in what is a sacred drama, a symbolic action or sacrament. Remember that the primary meaning of the 'blessed sacrament' is the celebration of the Mass. In that celebration things are done and proclaimed and sacred objects are employed. By this whole complex of word and action we celebrate the sacrament of the Paschal Mystery.

The quality of the liturgical act is of the first importance. The General Instruction is deeply concerned with quality. It contains regulations about the arrangement of the church for the celebration of Mass and the quality of the eucharistic bread and wine and other things employed in the celebration.

Structure and form of the celebration of the Mass

The General Instruction on the Roman Missal helps us to look intelligently at the way in which the celebration of Mass is structured. We come to Mass, we celebrate it, we look at it as one whole activity, all of which it is necessary to perform. Within that unity, however, it is possible to distinguish two main sections. These are usually known as the Liturgy of the Word and the Liturgy of the Eucharist. To these are added some introductory and concluding rites. The proclamation of the Word and the celebration of the eucharist are sometimes thought of as two 'tables of the Lord'. Perhaps it is just as good to think of the Mass as one 'table of the Lord' with two aspects. The Word of God is like the bread of the eucharist. It is Christ present among his people. It is proclaimed, broken and shared at *both* 'the table of the Word' *and* 'the table of the Eucharist'.

So it is necessary to consider both the major sections, Word and eucharist, together with the rites that form an important introduction to the whole Mass and those which conclude the celebration.

Introductory Rites

'To prepare ourselves to celebrate the sacred mysteries' is the purpose of all the rites of introduction. However, it is necessary to examine them more closely in order to discern various different approaches and methods of preparation. Here is a list of the introductory rites normally associated with Sunday Mass.

1. Opening song and entrance procession
2. Greeting
3. Introduction to the Mass
4. Penitential rite
5. Hymn: Glory to God in the highest
6. Opening prayer

These introductory rites serve two basic purposes: firstly, they assist the assembly to become an assembly. People leave home, make all the necessary arrangements to come to Mass and when they get there they need a centring or 'briefing' time. In any case, the first aim is simply to dispose those present to listen to the Word of God and to enter fully into the celebration of the liturgy. Secondly, it is the job of the introductory rites to announce the character of the celebration or feast celebrated. These two basic aims are what the rite means when the presiding minister asks people to prepare to celebrate the sacred mysteries.

All that is said or done in these opening moments should try to fulfil those two basic aims. Thus, for example, those who plan the liturgy should have chosen an opening song that truly sets the tone. In order to do this, they will have looked at all the core texts first, that is to say, the readings for the day, the prayers for the day and certainly the Preface to the Eucharistic Prayer which is going to be used.

The procession of entrance should be through the midst of the congregation. Preferably it should include the visible presence of the gospel book or the book containing the readings. The procession should give people the chance to see the elements of the liturgy and the identity of the presider. Lighted candles and incense may accompany the entrance procession; incense may also be used to venerate the altar when the gospel book is placed upon it. The whole process should be unhurried, a clear statement that now the assembly is complete and ready to do something of the greatest importance. To sing the entrance song helps further to invite the people into a larger whole and to draw their prayer and worship into one united act.

The presiding minister greets the people formally in the name of Christ. This is the sense of the greetings: 'The Lord be with you' and its alternatives in the Missal. These are formal ritual words; it is inappropriate to preface them (much more to replace them) with other more informal words of greeting. The words of introduction should be brief. Before the penitential rite, and again before the opening prayer the Missal asks for a pause for silent prayer. This enables the congregation to 'catch up' and gives it a chance to pray on its own before the presider 'collects' the prayer of the assembly in the opening prayer.

Adaptation

The opening rites are sometimes adapted in ways that fulfil their functions in a different manner. On the feast of the Presentation of Our Lord (2 February) and on Palm Sunday, the opening rites take the form of a procession. The intention is that this should be a real procession involving all, or a substantial number, of those present for the Mass. It is not intended that the procession should be simply a clerical perambulation of the church. Processions should start, ideally, from a place set apart from the church and go into the church where Mass is to be celebrated. The procession ends with the Gloria of the Mass and the opening prayer.

At a funeral Mass where the body enters the church at the beginning of Mass, the introductory rites are replaced by the entry of the body and the placing of the pall and/or other Christian symbols. This is followed by the opening prayer of the Mass.

When the sacrament of baptism is celebrated at Sunday Mass, the rite of reception of the child and the signing with the cross take the place of the penitential rite. They are followed by the Gloria (if appropriate) and the opening prayer.

On Ash Wednesday the introductory rites are abbreviated as the imposition of ashes takes the place of the penitential rite and is performed after the gospel and the homily.

On Sundays, particularly on the Sundays of Eastertide, the introductory rites may take the form of blessing and sprinkling holy water over the assembly. Once again they are followed by the Gloria and the opening prayer.

It is clear from the adaptations provided in the liturgical books that the opening rites are intended to be flexible, provided their overall purpose is achieved. Within the Missal there is a choice of opening greetings and forms for the penitential rite which may be used at different times. Penitential Rite C, for example, takes the form of a litany with the acclamation 'Kyrie eleison'. It would be appropriate on major feast days to use this third form instead of a more specifically penitential opening rite such as the 'I confess' which might be preferred, say, on the Sundays of Lent. It is possible to organize the opening rites of Mass in order to reflect the liturgical season and the atmosphere of the liturgy. The opening prayer always concludes the opening rites, whatever their form. Like the prayer over the gifts and the prayer after communion, the function of the opening prayer is to conclude a section of the liturgy, to mark a point of transition. As in the penitential rite, the opening prayer is to be preceded by a period of silent prayer.

The Liturgy of the Word

When the words of Scripture are proclaimed it is as if God speaks. God's Word is not so much 'message' as 'event'. 'By his word the heavens were made' (Psalm 33). For the Church the Word of God is a human person, for it is in Christ that 'the word was made flesh and dwelt among us' (John 1). The Liturgy of the Word, therefore, ought to be experienced as a real coming of Christ among his people – Christ whom we believe to be the incarnation of all God's purposes as they unfold in both Hebrew and Christian Scriptures. The Liturgy of the Word is a process of dialogue where the Church both listens and responds, hears and receives God the Word. This pattern of hearing and response enables interiorization and contemplation to take place. It shapes the structure of the Liturgy of the Word, which passes from reading into response psalm and from gospel into homily and intercession.

God's Word reminds us that we are God's people called to serve his creation. The homily exists to apply that Word to us here and now. Intercession is the priestly work of the assembly, bringing before God the needs of all to whom his Word is addressed.

The books for the Liturgy of the Word are the Lectionary and Book of Gospels. The Lectionary is simply the Scriptures arranged for liturgical use. It is, however, no random arrangement. Two principles have been used to arrange the Bible for proclamation at Sunday and weekday Mass: the assigning of each gospel to a particular year, and the harmonization of some or all of the readings at each Mass.

Let the gospel be heard

The four gospels are all different. We all know that John is somehow different from Matthew, Mark and Luke, but even the first three gospels themselves have their own differences. Each makes known in its own way the good news of Jesus Christ, the Son of God.

• Many people remember and treasure stories such as the Good

Samaritan, the Prodigal Son, Zacchaeus, and so on, but it comes as a surprise to many that these stories are only in the gospel of Luke.

- Many people remember the Sermon on the Mount but fewer realize that this is only found (as a complete collection of teaching) in Matthew's gospel. Again, if we compare the Beatitudes in Matthew and Luke, they will be seen to be different.
- Both Matthew and Luke have stories of Jesus' conception and birth. They are different stories. Mark has no birth narrative at all.

The Lectionary for Sunday and feast-day Masses allows each gospel to speak for itself. The Lectionary works on a three-year cycle of readings for Sundays and major feasts; the first of these years is dominated by the gospel of Matthew, the second by the gospel of Mark and the third by the gospel of Luke. The gospel of John is read in full every year.

Apart from the systematic reading of the synoptic gospels in Years A, B and C, the other readings in the Liturgy of the Word also deserve attention. Here, however, there is a difference between the way the Liturgy of the Word is treated on Sundays in Ordinary Time (when the vestments of the priest are green) and on other Sundays of the year (Advent, Christmas, Lent and Eastertide). When the vestments are green, it is usually the case that the Old Testament reading has been deliberately chosen to harmonize with the gospel. The second reading is chosen on a different basis and is a continuous reading from the letters of the New Testament, usually those of St Paul. So, on the 'green' Sundays the first reading and the gospel will be in some sort of relationship, the second reading will not be.

On the Sundays in Advent, Christmas and Lent it is usual that all three readings will in some way harmonize with one another. On those Sundays, it is also the case that the gospels may not always be from the gospel read in Year A, B or C. For example, the Third, Fourth and Fifth Sundays of Lent for Year A (the year of Matthew) are taken from the gospel of John.

On the Sundays from Easter to Pentecost the readings do not normally harmonize at all. This is because the first reading is always taken from the Acts of the Apostles, read in a semi-continuous basis; the second reading is usually from the Apocalypse; and the gospels are, in the first place, the Easter appearances of Jesus and, later on, the 'I am' sayings from John. As the time draws nearer to Pentecost, the gospels are taken from the Last Supper discourse and the so-called 'high priestly prayer' of Jesus in the gospel of John.

Homily

At all the Masses on Sundays and major feast days, the homily is obligatory. It is commended on others days (GIRM 42). The function of the homily has been discussed elsewhere in this book. Suffice it to say that it is one of the features of the Conciliar reform of the liturgy that the homily forms part of the Mass, and, in its position between the Liturgy of the Word and the Liturgy of the Eucharist, performs a bridging role for the people.

The general intercessions

The restoration of the general intercessions or the 'prayer of the faithful' in the order of Mass was once again a fruit of the Second Vatican Council. The directions given for the general intercessions are simple. Firstly, it is a universal prayer. It is the exercise of a priestly or intercessory ministry of the Church, a sharing in the universal prayer of Christ, for *all* creation, *all* humanity, *all* human need. Although space is given in the course of the prayer for local needs and local intentions, the thrust of the general intercessions is universal. Secondly, it is a prayer of supplication, not a prayer of thanksgiving. Petitions should be framed to reflect this. Thirdly, it is a prayer of the people, not of the minister who reads it. This means that petitions should be framed so that they are, in fact, *invitations* to the people to pray. They should run something like: 'Let us pray for ...'. The idea is that we are asking the whole congregation to pray for a particular need, preferably giving them a pause of a few seconds to do so, and then closing the petition with a short response. To have the reader direct a prayer to God on behalf of the congregation, rather than inviting the congregation themselves to pray, is not a 'prayer of the faithful'. It is customary for the priest to introduce the prayer with a few words. It is customary also to conclude the prayer with the Hail Mary immediately before the concluding collect recited by the priest.

The Liturgy of the Eucharist

'Christ took bread and the cup, broke it, gave it to his disciples saying, "Take and eat, this is my body; take and drink, this is the cup of my blood. Do this in memory of me." The Church has arranged the celebrations of the Eucharistic Liturgy to correspond to these words and actions of Christ' (GIRM 48).

The Liturgy of the Eucharist takes place at the altar, the Lord's table. Bread and wine are brought and prepared, the Eucharistic Prayer is proclaimed, bread is broken and shared among the participants together with the cup. These four actions are the Catholic eucharist.

Of these actions, the two most important are the Eucharistic Prayer and the sharing of the eucharistic bread and cup in Holy Communion. These are what Jesus told us to do in memory of him.

It would be possible to do all these actions except the Eucharistic Prayer without words. However, the developments of the rites over many centuries has added words to actions as the Church has deepened its understanding of what it is doing.

Preparation of the Gifts

> Preparation of the altar – cloths, books, chalice etc.
> Procession with bread and wine, presentation to the presider
> Prayer: 'Blessed are you . . .' with optional response
> Mixing of chalice and prayer: 'By the mystery . . .'
> Prayer: 'Blessed are you . . .' with optional response
> Prayer: 'Lord, we ask your . . .'
> Washing of hands and prayer: 'Lord, wash away . . .'
> Invitation: 'Pray, brothers and sisters . . .'
> Prayer over the gifts

Actually, this is quite a complicated set of rites, with various possible ways of their performance, from the very simple to the very elaborate. At the simplest, all the prayers are said quietly (the Missal envisages this as the norm) without any response until 'Pray, brothers and sisters . . .'. The whole action may be done in silence or during singing.

To do it simply like this is the best way, as this is merely a preparation, so that the Eucharistic Prayer may be better highlighted. The term 'offertory' has been dropped from the Roman Missal in favour of the word 'preparation'.

The preparation of the gifts may be accompanied by singing or instrumental music. The placing of the gifts on the altar may be accompanied by their censing; the censing of the altar and the people would then follow. At such a moment as this, it is important to stress actions, gestures and activity rather than words.

The Eucharistic Prayer

'The Eucharistic Prayer, a prayer of thanksgiving and sanctification, is the high point of the entire celebration. The meaning of the prayer is that the whole congregation joins Christ in acknowledging the works of God and offering the sacrifice' (GIRM 54). The Eucharistic Prayer represents the Church's own wording of the prayer of Jesus when he gave thanks and praise over the bread and cup.

Ancient tradition, going back beyond the time of Jesus and the apostles, makes the Eucharistic Prayer both a thanksgiving and a supplication. It is the function of the prayer to proclaim the wonderful works of God and to ask God, through the eucharist, to be faithful in the future to all that he has done in the past. The Eucharistic Prayer assumes that the mystery of our salvation is made present here and now in the eucharistic sacrifice, and that the future unfolding of God's purposes to their glorious end is also made present in the celebration of the eucharist. This pattern of past, present and future is one that all the Eucharistic Prayers manifest in some way. The pattern determines the very structure of the prayer itself.

The Eucharistic Prayer is the prayer of the whole Church, as the whole Church is manifested in the whole assembly gathered for Mass. The Eucharistic Prayer, like all prayers in the liturgy, is prayed in the first person plural, it is a 'we' prayer articulated by the ordained presider and responded to by the assembly.

The Eucharistic Prayer is also, as it were, the prayer of Christ who has offered himself for the salvation of all. The ordained presider articulates the prayer of the Church and the prayer of Christ at one and the same time. The assembly intervenes in the prayer to make the prayer of Christ its very own. The Eucharistic Prayer is not intended to be a monologue. It is a dialogue between God and God's people, between ministers and assembly. At pivotal points – beginning, middle, concluding doxology – the assembly sings acclamations which give shape and direction to the prayer.

Structure of the Eucharistic Prayer

1. Dialogue:	'The Lord be with you'/'Lift up your hearts'/'Let us give thanks to the Lord, our God'
2. Preface:	praise and thanksgiving for the mystery of salvation
3. First acclamation:	'Holy, holy, holy . . .'
4. Eucharistic Prayer I:	intercession and communion commemorations
II and III:	a bridging passage
IV:	continuation of thanksgiving
5. Invocation over the gifts:	'that they may become the body and blood of Christ'
6. Last Supper narrative	
7. Second acclamation:	'Mystery of faith'

8. Articulation of the eucharistic action:	'We offer you, in thanksgiving, this holy and living sacrifice'
9. Invocation of the Holy Spirit upon the Church:	'Grant that we who are nourished by his body and blood, may be filled with the Holy Spirit and become one body, one Spirit in Christ'
10. Eucharistic Prayer I:	prayer for the dead and second commemoration of saints
II, III + IV:	intercession for the whole church and for all the living and dead
11. Final Doxology:	that with all God's people we may praise God for ever, through and with and in Christ
12. Third Acclamation:	'Amen'

Breaking the eucharistic bread

The act of breaking the eucharistic bread is often lost on our congregations. Just one large 'host' is broken by the priest. The Roman Missal, however, says this about the eucharistic bread:

> The nature of the sign demands that the material for the Eucharistic celebration appear as actual food. The Eucharistic bread, even though unleavened and traditional in form, should therefore be made in such a way that the priest can break it and distribute the parts to at least some of the faithful. When the number of communicants is large, or other pastoral needs require it, small hosts may be used. The gesture of the breaking of the bread, as the Eucharist was called in apostolic times will more clearly show the Eucharist as a sign of unity and charity as the one bread is being distributed among the members of one family. (GIRM 283)

The New Testament refers to the 'breaking of bread' in both the Acts of the Apostles and in St Paul's first letter to the Corinthians. St Paul considers it an action of the deepest significance. 'Though there are many of us, we are one body, for we all share one loaf.' So the breaking of bread is a parable in action. It speaks of: 1. The unity and peace of Christ's faithful in the eucharist. 2. The need to be reconciled with one another around the table of the Lord.

The breaking of the bread

The Lord's Prayer

Prayer:	'Deliver us, Lord . . .'
The conclusion:	'For the kingdom . . .'
The rite of peace; prayer:	'Lord Jesus Christ . . .'
Greeting and sign of peace	
Litany:	'Lamb of God . . .' to be sung while the eucharistic bread is being broken
Invitation to communion:	'This is the Lamb of God . . .'

The rites that precede communion may be looked at in two ways. Firstly, they may be seen as an expression of the God-given unity of Christ's people in the one broken bread. Secondly, as a penitential ritual these rites act out our sorrow for sin against the background of God's will for unity among his people. Both of these approaches are an essential prelude to communion which seals the bond of unity, forgives and heals the members and opens to all the promise of the kingdom that is to come. The bread must be broken in order for oneness in communion to take place. The paradox of broken bread is the sign of Christ's will for unity and peace in the Church.

Communion

The eucharist is Christ giving his body and blood. It is the mode of his saving presence here and now. Eucharistic communion sets the seal on the sacrifice of the Lord which is the sacrifice of the Church.

Jesus asked his disciples both to eat and to drink. Both the body and the blood of Christ are the sacrifice. Both, therefore, should be received in order to participate fully in the mystery. Communion from the chalice is not an option for the few.

The nature of the sign requires that we share the gifts offered at the Mass which is being celebrated. The Church has, for many hundreds of years, urged priests and people to give communion from the gifts consecrated at the Mass, not from what was reserved in the tabernacle from a previous celebration. Communion from the reserve breaks the unity between sacrifice and communion in the one sacramental celebration.

Communion brings to fulfilment what has been proclaimed in the Liturgy of the Word. The gospel is proclaimed: the gospel is received too as bread and cup. The gift is the sacrament of the gospel, a sign in which the meaning of the words appears. To make this clear, on many occasions the texts used for the communion songs in the Missal are drawn from the gospel read at that Mass.

Jesus' command 'Take, eat, drink. Do this in memory of me' is observed most fully in communion. For those who participate, communion is the culmination of the Mass.

The Missal envisages communion taking place as a procession. It may be thought of as another 'acted parable' in which the assembly makes a pilgrimage to communion in order to express itself as *a communion*. It is important to distinguish a procession from what normally seems to happen at communion in Catholic churches. The arrangement of buildings with rows of pews or chairs makes processional movement difficult when that movement is to be accomplished by a very large number of people. Chairs or pews are intended for sitting and listening. It would be an interesting challenge to an architect or church planner to devise an internal layout for a church building to accommodate regular and large-scale processions.

The song that the Missal provides as the processional chant during communion, frequently based on the gospel of the day, gives us an idea of the kind of thing that should be selected to accompany the procession. Processions are best accompanied by songs, chants or choruses for which people do not have to use books because the words are easily memorable, oft repeated, and simple. Song binds together those who are making the procession, the purpose also of the song at the opening of Mass. The fact of a procession at communion underlines the truth that communion itself is not to be seen as the isolated act of many individuals but as the single act of a gathered community. The point was made in discussing the communion rites that the mystery of the broken bread, the bread divided into many parts, is, by a paradox, the mystery of the unity and peace of Christ's Church. A procession is a common activity which needs to be distinguished from what frequently happens in Catholic churches, namely, an individual approach by a large number of people to an individual act of communion. The fact that many congregations prefer silence to song at this moment should make us all the more concerned to stress the communal nature of communion as opposed to its portrayal as a moment of prayer for individuals.

The response to the words 'The Body of Christ' is 'Amen'. This word is to be construed, firstly, as a word of welcome and acceptance of what is being offered and, secondly, as a credal statement, a statement that we believe in the reality of what is being offered to us. What we receive is truly the body and blood of Christ, but the body and blood of Christ that can be discerned on at least two different levels. We receive the bread of which Jesus spoke, 'This is my body', and we also receive the body of Christ which is Christ's own Church, or what the Church is called to be. 'Amen' has to be understood as a response to all these things. This brings to mind St Augustine's well-known recommendation to the newly-baptized, that 'Amen' was an act of affirmation of their own deepest identity as themselves the body of Christ.

Concluding rites

Eucharist, the celebration of Mass, is not an end in itself. It is a sacrament of mission and of future glory. The Church is called to live out the mystery of Christ in this world and to journey towards the eschatological fullness of that mystery.

The concluding rites of the Mass focus upon this twofold theme. However, the feature that most clearly illustrates the 'transitory' nature of the whole celebration is the simple brevity of the rites after communion. In the Roman liturgy they are very simple – the post-communion prayer, notices and information, blessing and dismissal. There is, of course, nothing in the Roman Missal about the singing of a final song to conclude Mass.

The prayer after communion

As has been noted before, the function of the three presidential prayers of the Mass (the opening prayer, the prayer over the offerings and the post-communion prayer) is to conclude a major section of the liturgy and to prepare for the next section. The post-communion prayers of the Roman Rite point either towards the mission of the Church in this world or towards its eternal destiny. A study of any group of post-communion prayers in the Missal will reveal these characteristics.

In the revised Roman Mass the time deemed most appropriate for the giving of notices and information concerning parish events is at the end of Mass, after the post-communion prayer.

The Roman Mass ends with a blessing and dismissal, or it may end with a prayer over the people followed by a blessing and dismissal. The Roman Missal provides different forms for the ending of Mass. The common form is a simple blessing made with the sign of the cross and accompanying formula. During penitential seasons and at other times, the 'prayer over the people' may be recited with the priest stretching out his hands over the assembly and giving the simple blessing after the assembly has responded 'Amen'. The third form to be used on more solemn occasions is what is known as a solemn blessing. This consists of three parts concluded with an 'Amen'; a fourth element is the blessing formula itself. There are, in addition, a number of simpler blessing texts based on biblical texts from the Old and New Testaments.

The whole idea of ending the celebration of Mass with a blessing before the dismissal is a new one. The blessing, the descendant of an informal priestly or episcopal blessing given as the presider left the church, was given after the dismissal in the old Roman Rite. This is an indication that in earlier times no blessing was given at the end of Mass – indeed we know that in some parts of Europe, if a blessing was given, it was in fact given before people came up to communion. It may be that the idea of ending Mass with a single prayer and dismissal was intended to make the Church more aware that in fact the eucharist has not truly ended, in that its missionary and eschatological dimensions are still to be lived out and fulfilled.

Music in the Mass

(See Chapter 7 for a full treatment of the subject of music.)

The importance of song in the celebration of Mass cannot be over-emphasized. However, developments in this country have given a false impression as to the exact meaning of such a statement. From the time of Pius X, the liturgical movement sought to restore active participation in a sung liturgy as the norm for Catholic liturgy and to effect this kind of liturgical participation. With the emergence of the 'dialogue Mass' in the mid-1920s, a new form of liturgical participation was invented and the congregation recited, in the spoken voice, the responses of the server. With the Second Vatican Council and the coming of liturgy in the vernacular, the assumption was made (at least in the UK) that English liturgy would be spoken liturgy. If there was to be music at all, it would consist in the singing of hymns. In this way, the so-called 'four-hymn Mass' became virtually a norm.

The visions of the liturgical movement and the Council are different, however. The 1967 Instruction on sacred music (which is reproduced in part in the GIRM) emphasizes the importance of *singing the Mass* as opposed to merely singing *at* Mass. Clearly the intention is that every part of the Mass should be sung. Priority, however, is to be given to acclamations and to those parts in which the congregation dialogue with the presiding minister. This means that hymns, as we are accustomed to sing them, do not in fact have top priority. At a Mass where there is to be little singing, the priority should be to sing, firstly, the acclamations in the Eucharistic Prayer ('Holy, holy', 'Christ has died' and the concluding 'Amen') and, secondly, the gospel acclamation. At a Mass where there is rather more than the minimal content of song, further priority should be given to the responsorial psalm, the 'Lamb of God' and other texts of the Ordinary. At Masses where there is to be a maximum amount of singing, songs are also sung at the entry, the preparation of the gifts and at communion. This, of course, looks like a total reversal of the musical priorities that have been observed in many Catholic churches for the last thirty years. In fact, the emphasis on liturgy as inherently a *sung* activity, or an activity in which music and song play an important role, is nothing new. It is the concept of liturgy in the spoken voice that is a new arrival on the scene. In the Middle Ages and right up to recent times, the liturgy was either chanted out loud or recited in a whisper, as a dialogue between priest and server. Furthermore, it is clear that the worship of all the major world religions is celebrated to the accompaniment of song or chant. This suggests the considerable power that singing can exert. GIRM draws attention to the power of song to bind an assembly together. Clearly, if liturgical prayer is to ascend to God, as it were, it should ascend as one unit, not as a medley of individual prayers uttered by each participant. Song has been the provider of such 'binding' since the beginning. It should, of course, have certain characteristics. Good models are given in some of the simpler ancient chants of the Roman Rite, such as Sanctus XVIII in the *Graduale Romanum* which virtually chants the text on a single note with variations. This, and other chants of the same simple kind, offer a means of participation accessible to all, even to those who say they cannot 'sing'. Much new composition is needed to provide the liturgy with appropriate song. We have also a very rich tradition of elaborate choral music written for the service of the liturgy, and perhaps we are beginning to realize that this music is not inappropriate for the celebration of Mass in the reformed Roman Rite, provided that its positioning in the structure of the rite is carefully articulated.

To conclude this short section, it should be noted that singing and music are not ornamental features of the liturgy. They are part of liturgy's very essence, a binding force for the assembly's prayer. Music and song serve the liturgy and help it to achieve its proper aim – the glory of God and the sanctification of God's people.

DOCUMENTATION AND BIBLIOGRAPHY

Constitution on the Liturgy, ch. 21.

General Instruction on the Roman Missal (GIRM), 1–5, 7, 8, 48–56.

J. D. Crichton, *Christian Celebration: Understanding the Mass* (new edition: London: Geoffrey Chapman, 1992).

J. D. Crichton, *A Short History of the Mass* (London: CTS, 1983).

Geoffrey Cuming, *He Gave Thanks: An Introduction to the Eucharistic Prayer* (*Grove Liturgical Study* no. 28; Nottingham: Grove Books, 1981).

Johannes H. Emminghaus, *The Eucharist: Essence, Form and Celebration* (Collegeville, MN: The Liturgical Press, 1978).

Alan Griffiths, *Focus on the Eucharistic Prayer* (Bury St Edmunds: Kevin Mayhew, 1988).

Lawrence J. Johnson, *The Word and Eucharist Handbook* (San Jose, CA: Resource Publications, 1986).

Ralph Keifer, *To Give Thanks and Praise: General Instruction on the Roman Missal with Commentary for Musicians and Pastors* (Washington, DC: National Association of Pastoral Musicians, 1980).

A. G. Martimort (ed.), *The Church at Prayer*, vol. II (London: Geoffrey Chapman, 1986).

D. A. Withey, *Catholic Worship* (Bury St Edmunds: Kevin Mayhew, 1990), ch. 11.

Unit 4

JULIE ANNE DONNELLY SND

THE LITURGICAL YEAR: LIVING THE PASCHAL MYSTERY

1. General overview

The Second Vatican Council decreed the revision of the liturgical year to 'nourish the piety of the faithful who celebrate the mysteries of Christian redemption, especially the paschal mystery' (SC 107). Pope Paul VI expanded this statement when he introduced the revised calendar: 'The purpose of the liturgical year and the revision of its norms is to allow the faithful through their faith, hope and love, to share more deeply in the whole mystery of Christ as it unfolds throughout the year', i.e. to live this Paschal Mystery of Christ's death and resurrection with which we became personally identified by our baptism (cf. Romans 6:3–11). The view of Christian life as a Passover is founded on this paschal character of Christian baptism. Christian life is a passage through death to life, our individual and communal participation in the unique passing over of Christ. Each individual's natural cycle is conception, birth, childhood, adolescence, maturity, old age, death, birth into eternity, and the mysteries of our redemption in Christ are grafted on to this natural life cycle. Each stage involves us in a dying to what has been and a rising to something new; a growth from immaturity to maturity; from inexperience to experience; from ignorance to wisdom; from death to life. This has to come about in our own specific historical and geographical setting – so Christians have a particular view of time.

God's wondrous deeds of salvation were carried out at a definite time: 'When the appointed time came, God sent his Son, born of a woman' (Galatians 4:4). Our salvation is structured on recurring rhythms of human experience: daily, weekly, monthly and annual. Our annual liturgical calendar structures our time for us in relation to worship. Time is part of the scientific world of accurate measurement to fractions of a second, as in Olympic scoring. It is also the stuff of poetry. Many ancient peoples saw time as a recurring cycle in which we are trapped, condemned to repeating rituals endlessly. The revelation to, and through, Israel that there existed one Lord who was not only eternally present and in touch with the whole of creation, but who also had a plan for this creation, replaced the view of time as an endless cycle, with a linear concept. Time is like an arrow moving to a given target, a line with a beginning and an end, from creation to final judgement.

The Septuagint and the New Testament use the Greek word *chronos* to express this idea of linear time at the end of which God's judgement will definitively occur and salvation will be decisively completed as promised. We derive 'chronology' and related words, which describe time as an ordered sequence, from *chronos*.

For describing specific points in time, such as propitious moments, the Greeks used the word *kairos*. In the New Testament, *kairos* means a decisive moment of salvation demanding decision by individuals and judgement by God. **The** *kairos* was the Passover of Jesus from death on the cross to risen glory. For each Christian, the ultimate *kairos* is the moment of biological death and passover into the fullness of risen glory with Christ. But every individual's personal story of salvation is about a series of such decisive moments throughout life. Ongoing conversion involves our positive responses to such growth points. A certain rhythmic tension exists between *chronos*, the orderly sequence of our lives, and *kairos*, the special decisive moments. This is symbolically expressed in our liturgical calendar which programmes our Christian year into seasons of special festivity and long stretches of ordinary time. We become a people shaped by our liturgy when we learn to live by this liturgical calendar and to sanctify *our* time by inserting our fleeting moments into the everlasting Christ (cf. the Paschal candle at the Easter Vigil).

Foundation

There is also tension and mystery in the intersection of our time and God's eternity. The advent of the eternal Word into our time has given human history a totally new and mysterious dimension. We can only speak in such temporal terms as past, present and future, but these are brought together in our liturgy. We celebrate liturgy to remember the Paschal Mystery which happened in the past, to point us to the future, and as a way of actualizing the power of those events in the present. The liturgical year is a calendar of critical turning-points in the life of the people of God in which the power of the Paschal Mystery is released *today* into our lives. It is not a search for the historical Jesus who lived 2,000 years ago, but a celebration of the risen

Christ who calls us to salvation *now* (cf. the use of 'today' in the Christmas liturgies, 'This is the night' in the *Exsultet*, etc.).

The Paschal Mystery

The revision of the liturgical year, therefore, laid special emphasis on the Paschal Mystery as central to Christian life and to Christian celebration. Pope Paul VI stressed that liturgy and life are intimately linked and that the Paschal Mystery is central to both:

> The thrust of pastoral activity centred on the liturgy is to give expression to the paschal mystery in people's lives ...
> accomplished by faith and by the sacraments of faith, especially by baptism, by the sacred mystery of the eucharist ... and by the cycle of celebrations in which, throughout the Church's year, the paschal mystery of Christ is unfolded.

The 'cycle of celebrations' of seasons and feasts of the Church's year, therefore, is officially regarded as an extremely important means of spiritual development, liturgical formation and awakening the faithful to their vocation as God's people, especially by keeping Christ's Paschal Mystery at the very centre of their Christian lives.

'Paschal Mystery' is theological shorthand for the passion, death, resurrection, ascension and glorification of Jesus which liberates people from the death of sin to life in God. Christ's work of redemption is brought about in us by our celebration of liturgy. This draws Christians into his dying and rising by the communal act of remembering what God did and does for his people in Christ. Israel's spirituality was (and is) based upon their remembering together the wonderful works of God in their history. Their covenant relationship with God, initiated in the Exodus event, was experienced and forged anew by successive generations in their liturgical remembering – weekly on the sabbath and annually at Passover. So it is for Christians as well. As heirs of Israel, their Passover is part of our history too. Every spring, the liturgy makes it clear that we are expected to enter into the whole Passover event as participants. The *Exsultet* states categorically that 'This is the night when ...' the Exodus took place; when the pillar of fire destroyed the darkness of sin – when Christ accomplished these things in their full reality in his Paschal Mystery.

The process of sanctification is a process of becoming, of being freed from the slavery of sin and made holy through being repeatedly drawn into Christ's Paschal Mystery through the liturgy. This process is rooted in time, in the whole event of redemption which began with the Exodus of Israel from Egypt, was completed and fulfilled by the Paschal

Mystery of Jesus and occurs today in us through the liturgical celebration of the sacraments and the seasons and feasts of the Church's year. Hence devotion to the Paschal Mystery is central to our lives as Christians. It is the very heart of the liturgy and the entire liturgical year grows out of it.

Sanctifying time

Time is a gift of our creator. Its divisions are determined by cosmic elements, particularly sun and moon which give us the day, the month and the year. Our seven-day week, however, is more directly a biblical and God-given division of days; part of revelation (Exodus 31:17). The week cannot be read in the sky!

THE DAY. Before artificial heat and light were available, people's lives were largely controlled by sunrise and sunset. The Church's ancient tradition is to sanctify the day by prayer at these important pivotal moments, and also during the day and after nightfall. The 'Liturgy of the Hours' is a communal prayer designed to involve the entire community in giving thanks and praise to God. Morning Prayer recalls Christ's resurrection, consecrates our day to God and praises him for the beauty of creation. Evening Prayer thanks him for the gift of the day and for his love. Prayer during the day, and Night Prayer, ask for help during the day and for protection during the night. The prayer of the Church complements the daily celebration of the eucharist. 'To the different hours of the day, the liturgy of the Hours extends the praise and thanksgiving, the memorial of the mysteries of salvation, the petitions and foretaste of heavenly glory that are present in the eucharistic mystery' (GILH 12).

THE WEEK is sanctified by our assembling on its first day, the Lord's Day, and celebrating the memorial of Christ's Paschal Mystery. This makes the following six working days sanctified from the start. Our celebration on the first day of the week recalls the day when God began the work of creation. As Christians, we are working to renew the face of the earth, fulfilling our role in creation.

THE YEAR is sanctified by our Christian remembering of the cycle of salvation history. The liturgical year is a continual anamnesis or remembering, when past, present and future intersect in the *now* of today: 'Now is the acceptable time: now is the day of salvation' (2 Corinthians 6:2). The way to live as a Catholic Christian is not learnt from books, but by living the cycle of the liturgical year – year after year after year ... This liturgical year releases the power of the Paschal Mystery into our lives today. It was revised precisely so that we could 'share more deeply in the whole mystery of Christ as it unfolds throughout the year' (Pope Paul VI, *Inter Oecumenici*). In Christ, all time is a feast; all days are the Lord's and we give thanks 'always and everywhere'.

2. Principles of the liturgical calendar

Theologically and historically, the Church's calendar of seasons, feasts and ordinary time grew very gradually from the initial weekly celebration of the Paschal Mystery on the 'first day of the week', as mentioned in the Acts of the Apostles. The special annual celebration of Easter took form much more slowly, but was established in both Western and Eastern Churches by the fourth century. The absolute central position of the Paschal Mystery is the Church's primary principle for the liturgical calendar.

The revised liturgical year includes two major seasons. The Easter season begins on Ash Wednesday and ends ninety-six days later on Pentecost Sunday. The Christmas season, an annual commemoration and celebration of Christ's first coming, begins on the First Sunday of Advent (with Evening Prayer I) and ends on the Baptism of the Lord. These two festal seasons together occupy about a third of the year. The remaining thirty-three or thirty-four weeks are called Ordinary Time. This begins on the Monday after the feast of the Baptism of the Lord, is interrupted by the Easter season, then continues from the Monday after Pentecost Sunday until the eve of the First Sunday of Advent. Ordinary Time and the two seasons form the Proper of Time, or Temporal Cycle. This is pre-eminent. Saints' feasts, of secondary importance, form the Sanctoral Cycle. They have dates according to the civil calendar and the cycle runs concurrently with the Temporal Cycle. When dates coincide, the latter has priority.

A. The Lord's Day

Catholic consciousness of Sunday's significance needs re-awakening. Celebrating the Lord's Day involves much more than spending an hour in church; much more than regarding it as the day 'when we've got to go to Mass'. It is the weekly feast day. 'Sunday is the foundation and core of the whole liturgical year ... the year of Christian life itself.'

Sunday is the 'heart of the liturgical year' historically, theologically and pastorally. Historically, Sunday is the oldest element in the Christian calendar, the original feast day, as the New Testament makes clear (see John 20:19–23; 20:24–29; Acts 20:7–12). It is the nucleus around and out of which the feasts and seasons of the Church's year evolved.

Theologically, Sunday retains in itself the kernel of the Christian mystery, dying and rising, the whole economy of salvation. Pastorally, it is the day when the local church assembles for worship, gathers together visibly as church.

Originally the Church celebrated the memorial of Christ's dying and rising in the evening, at the time when many of the post-resurrection appearances of the risen Lord took place. The focus was on the encounter with the Lord, rather than on the actual resurrection itself (which presumably took place in the early morning). These post-resurrection meals seem to have been the origin of the observance of Sunday as the pre-eminent day for celebrating the eucharist. As St Peter claimed: 'We are the witnesses – we have eaten and drunk with him after his resurrection from the dead' (see Acts 10:41). Shared exposure to the risen Christ and shared experience of the action of his Spirit brought a new people of God into being. For these early Christians, the Sunday evening asssembly was the time and place when they expected to see him again. They gathered in expectation of what was to come, aware of belonging to a living community which drew them to participate in the mystery, the visible expression of their unity. The principle which prevailed at this time might be described as: 'No Sunday without the eucharist; no eucharist without an assembly of the people.' Sunday was the weekly celebration of the Paschal Mystery and the day of the eucharistic assembly. Until AD 321 it was a working day, too.

Gradually, Christians began to celebrate annually one particular Sunday as the Christian Pasch. This development of Easter resulted more from the need to complete the long initiation process for new adult members than simply to celebrate an annual, as well as a weekly, memorial of the Paschal Mystery.

In revising the liturgical calendar, the Church has tried to reinstate this original Christian attitude to Sunday. The Fathers of Vatican II, drawing on early tradition, call Sunday 'the eighth day': 'The Church celebrates the paschal mystery every eighth day.' This image of Sunday as the eighth day of a seven-day week lifts it out of our usual understanding of time and draws us forward into that final never-ending day which is eternity. It celebrates the life that is to come. So Christians assemble on this day as the first fruits of the age that is to come and celebrate their redemption and their hope of eternity with eucharistic thanksgiving. With its assembly, its proclamation of the Word and its breaking of bread, Sunday, the eighth day, is, so to speak, a post-resurrection appearance of the risen Christ. The Sunday celebration of the eucharist should stand out as the principal liturgy of the week, the gathering of the local church.

Sunday should not be obscured by special themes and intentions which shift attention to our needs or to what we are doing for the

Lord, rather than concentrating on what he is doing for us. 'Other celebrations, unless of truly great importance, must not have precedence over Sunday.' There is a persistent tendency to attach days of special prayer to particular Sundays and 'themes' to Sunday Masses, e.g. vocations, youth, peace ... Such themes should never overshadow the liturgical and spiritual significance of the Sunday readings and the flow of the liturgical year. Celebrating the Lord's Supper on the Lord's Day is pre-eminently the celebration of the Paschal Mystery with the local assembly of Christ's present-day disciples. The Council has tried to bring us to a much fuller appreciation of Sunday as *the* day for the Christian community.

B. The seasons

The Paschal Triduum

The culmination of the entire liturgical year is the supreme celebration of the Paschal Mystery in the Easter Triduum. The preparatory period, Lent, ends quietly on Holy Thursday evening and the Church enters upon *the three days*, Good Friday, Holy Saturday and Easter Sunday, counted, according to Jewish practice, from sunset to sunset. The Evening Mass of the Lord's Supper on Holy Thursday is really the first liturgical event of Good Friday. The Triduum begins with the Evening Mass of the Lord's Supper and ends with Evening Prayer II on Easter Sunday (GNLYC 19).

The rites of Holy Thursday evening, Good Friday and the Easter Vigil are *one* liturgy, not three separate celebrations. There is no formal dismissal of the assembly at the end of the liturgies on Holy Thursday and Good Friday. Each time the assembly re-gathers, the one liturgy continues. The presider welcomes the people on Holy Thursday evening and dismisses them on Easter Sunday morning at the close of the Vigil Mass: 'Go, the Mass is ended, Alleluia! Alleluia!' Once the Triduum has begun, no other sacraments are celebrated, for the whole Church is caught up in a climactic annual celebration of the dying and rising of Christ. This is made actual by the baptizing of those being initiated into the Church after their RCIA journeying, especially through Lent. These three days of the Christian Passover are for us days of death, rest and resurrection.

Holy Thursday: Good Friday Eve

Holy Thursday's liturgy is the start of Easter (GNLYC 19). The Triduum is the annual Passover of the whole parish community – not merely an historical representation of Jesus' last meal, death and resurrection. The Holy Thursday liturgy reminds us in poignant fashion that our own passing-over from death to life in Jesus is known and shown by our service to one another. The power of this celebration lies in its unique gestures symbolizing what it means in practice for us to die and rise in Christ. Footwashing reminds us of our calling to do this; of our need to have it done for us; and how we die and rise in such washing and being washed.

Holy Thursday's rites introduce the entire Triduum, striking the keynote in the entry antiphon: 'We should glory in the cross of Our Lord Jesus Christ, for he is our salvation, our life and our resurrection; through him we are saved and made free.' The celebration consists of a Liturgy of the Word, followed by the Washing of Feet, the Liturgy of the Eucharist and the procession to transfer the communion hosts for Good Friday to their place of reservation. This is the one occasion when it is recommended that 'gifts for the poor' be carried to the altar along with the bread and wine at the presentation of gifts – all part of what this liturgy has to teach us about loving and serving others.

Good Friday

'Let the paschal fast be kept sacred. It should be observed everywhere on Good Friday, and where possible, on Holy Saturday.' The duty of fasting on Good Friday is incumbent on all adult Catholics. While not obligatory, this fast is highly recommended for Holy Saturday, too. This Easter fast is part of the death/resurrection focus of the Triduum and is quite different from the Lenten disciplinary fast. The Paschal fast is rather 'the excited nervous fasting of anticipation . . . like that of bride and groom before the wedding'. Those already baptized fast alongside the catechumens as they make their final preparations to receive baptism into the death of Jesus. From Holy Thursday evening until the end of the Vigil, we are too excited to eat. As already mentioned, this Paschal fast is also a fast from the sacraments.

Liturgically, on Good Friday, the cross is the centre of our prayer. It sums up the struggle between death and life. Veneration of the cross originated in Jerusalem after the true cross was found, and was part of the Good Friday liturgy there in the fourth century. Later on, when fragments of the true cross were made available in other cities, the practice of veneration spread. It reached Rome by the seventh century and thence went north through Europe. The chant 'Behold the wood of the cross' was already part of the liturgy by then. It is the cross itself, without a corpus, that is the symbol stressed by the liturgical texts and by the movements of the rite which focus on the wood itself, on the tree. The cross is the tree of life for us and the special homage given to the cross on this day closely resembles the veneration normally given to the reserved sacrament.

The Good Friday liturgy is named in the Sacramentary as the 'Celebration of the Lord's Passion'. The rite begins with absolutely silent prayer which is followed by a Liturgy of the Word (Scripture reading, homily and intercessions) and the veneration of the cross, and concludes with a simple communion service. The liturgy ends, as it began, in silence. As this is the central part of the one Triduum liturgy, there is no welcome at the beginning and no dismissal at the end.

Maintaining a prayerful atmosphere throughout Good Friday and on Holy Saturday needs such provision as the opportunity to gather for the Office of Readings, the Stations of the Cross and Taizé-style prayer around the cross. In today's ecumenical climate, Good Friday is often an occasion for joint prayer by all local Christian Churches.

Holy Saturday

Holy Saturday, like Good Friday, is a day without sacramental liturgy. From sunset on Good Friday to sunset on Holy Saturday we keep watch. These hours should be marked by ongoing prayer, especially for and with the elect preparing for baptism. The RCIA states that those who are preparing for baptism 'should rest from their ordinary work as far as possible, spend the time in prayer and recollection of mind and fast according to their ability'. The Sacramentary describes this day in rather historical terms: 'On Holy Saturday, the Church waits at the Lord's tomb meditating on his suffering and death.' The key word is 'waits'. The Catholic's inner movement all day is towards the Vigil. The final hours of the fast are filled with the excitement of the approaching proclamation of resurrection, baptism and the eucharist. The fasting has included fasting from sacraments. We need this time to ponder anew all that is meant by dying and rising with Jesus, the central mystery of our salvation. As we journey through our individual lives, we learn by experience that a 'dying' has to precede a better, fuller life. The Easter Triduum is far from being just a remembrance of events that occurred nearly two thousand years ago. It is immediate. It is for us now and today, the whole mystery of the Passover presence of the living God in us and in the people of God gathered together as Church.

The Easter Vigil

We gather together on this night of nights to celebrate the death and rising of Jesus in which we share through baptism and eucharist. The liturgy consists of four major rites: the Service of Light; the Proclamation of the Word; the Celebration of Baptism and the Liturgy of the Eucharist.

The Vigil begins outside in the darkness. Then the light is solemnly kindled and quickly overcomes the dark. The assembly processes into church behind this 'pillar of fire' and their individual candles are lit from the great Paschal candle ready for the announcement of Easter in the singing of the *Exsultet*; it is the Pasch. Seated, the assembly listens and responds to the stories that make this night what it is: creation; Abraham and Isaac; the Exodus dryshod through the waters; the visions of the prophets; Paul's great affirmation of the resurrection and the gospel account of the empty tomb. All this lays the foundation for celebrating the sacraments of initiation. The emphasis is on water and on those about to be baptized. It involves those already baptized in renewing their personal commitment, before all share in the eucharistic banquet 'when the whole church is called to the table which the Lord has prepared for his people through his death and resurrection'. For our communion thanksgiving we proclaim with St Paul: 'Christ has become our paschal sacrifice; let us feast with the unleavened bread of sincerity and truth' (1 Corinthians 5:7–8).

Lent/Eastertime

In our northern hemisphere, the seasonal pattern of nature helps us to a better understanding of Lent and Eastertime. During the weeks of March and April, the grey weariness of winter gradually gives way to the new life and light of spring. Dead-looking winter trees and bushes become transformed into living branches. Usually by Easter Sunday, fresh green leaves show forth the rebirth of nature. This annual transformation of nature speaks to Christians of our spiritual need for renewal and change. For this to happen in us, we need the preparatory period of Lent.

Lent

Lent came into being as the season of more intense preparation of the catechumens for reception of the sacraments of initiation at Easter. Today, the RCIA is helping to restore this approach to Lent as a journey to Easter with those preparing for baptism. Historically, when the flow of adult converts ceased, Lent became a time when those Christians who had sinned seriously, but wanted to return to the Christian community, were prepared by penance and fasting for reconciliation on Holy Thursday. At the beginning of Lent, as a sign of their sorrow, they had ashes sprinkled on their heads and dressed in sackcloth. In time, all the faithful, too, received ashes on the first day of Lent, as a sign that each and every one is a sinner.

Today, both the baptismal and the penitential elements are present in Lent. GNLYC 27 states:

> Lent is a preparation for the celebration of Easter. The Lenten liturgy disposes both catechumens and the faithful to celebrate the paschal mystery: catechumens, through the several stages of Christian initiation; the faithful, through reminders of their own baptism and through penitential practices.

So Lent has a twofold aspect, baptismal and penitential, and functions as a preparation for the Paschal Triduum. Lent is not an end in itself, but a passage, a journey we have to make together to the profound celebration of the risen Lord at Easter. But the joy of Easter is not just 'applause' because Christ has made it out of the valley of death to new never-ending life; it is *we* who have to make this passage. We 'die with Christ to rise with him' – this is what Easter celebrates. So on Ash Wednesday the whole Christian family sets out on a journey 'from ashes to Easter' – indeed 'from ashes to fire', since Pentecost is the conclusion of the Lent/Easter season.

Four phases can be discerned in the season of Lent: Ash Wednesday and the following three days form a solemn prelude to the season; from the First Sunday to Saturday of the fourth week the flow of the Scripture readings and the penitential rites directs our thoughts; from the Fifth Sunday onwards attention is increasingly focused on the passion of Christ; Passion Sunday and the following three days form a postlude to Lent and immediate preparation for the Triduum. These days are given the highest liturgical precedence so that the faithful will not be distracted from the final preparations for the Triduum. They open with the solemn celebration of Christ's entrance into Jerusalem to accomplish his Passover. The Church recalls this on Passion Sunday by a procession with palms hailing Christ as king. Palms symbolize the real message of this liturgy: that we are fickle, like those who acclaimed Jesus as king but called for his crucifixion a few days later. In the liturgy, the joyous procession is followed by the solemn proclamation of the passion. The palms, taken home and kept visible for the rest of the year, are a daily reminder that although we are fickle, we do desire to be loyal to Christ our king. They can also be regarded as the first signs of Christ's victory.

Eastertime

Just as the Easter Triduum is one liturgy spread over three days, so Eastertime is one celebration spread over fifty days. 'The fifty days between Easter Sunday and Pentecost are celebrated as one feast day.' This is a continuous celebration of the whole redemptive mystery, including the glorification of Christ, the sending of the Holy Spirit and our participation in the mystery through faith, baptism and eucharist. The Paschal period celebrates in a special way the presence of the risen Lord in his Church – Christ the bridegroom, risen and re-united with his bride, the Church. The Paschal candle symbolizes that presence and these fifty days, from Easter to Pentecost, are the honeymoon time. Christ's presence, here and now, in the Church is celebrated and made actual in the liturgy.

The keynote of Eastertime is joy – an anticipation and foretaste of heavenly joy. The characteristic expression of this joy is the repeated singing of 'Alleluia!' in the liturgy. However, this joy does not eliminate the memory of the passion. The risen Christ retained the visible signs of the wounds in his hands and side. The Paschal candle, too, has five nails embedded in it. Easter joy is not incompatible with suffering, both for the Church and for the individual Christian.

Liturgically, there are three phases in Eastertime, but these internal variations in the rhythm of the season should never obscure its unity as the great Fifty Days. The octave of Easter is the first eight days, each of which is a solemnity and raises us into the joy of the whole season. At the time of the adult catechumenate in Rome, these particular days were a period of post-baptismal instruction for the neophytes and this has influenced the prayer formulas and the choice of Scripture readings. The RCIA is reviving this period as one for deeper initiation of the newly-baptized into the community of the faithful. In the middle section, the Sunday gospels strongly colour the season. The first three Sundays relate post-resurrection appearances of Christ; the Fourth Sunday dwells on the Good Shepherd and the final three Sundays draw on the priestly prayer of Jesus from John's Gospel. The final days are those from Ascension Thursday to Pentecost. During these nine days we are called to pray 'together with Mary the Mother of Jesus and with his disciples' for the Holy Spirit. Eastertime, the Fifty Days, ends with Pentecost. The work of our redemption is accomplished and the Paschal Mystery of Christ's dying and rising continues in our lives – as Easter Preface IV proclaims: 'a new age has dawned . . . man is once again made whole'.

Advent/Christmastide

ADVENT comes at the end of the civil calendar year, but is the beginning of our liturgical calendar. Similarly, it embraces both the beginning of Christ's coming, the incarnation, and its future end, the coming of Christ in glory. So Advent has a twofold character: 'as a season to prepare for Christmas when Christ's first coming is remembered and as a season when that remembrance directs the mind and heart to await Christ's second coming at the end of time' (GNLYC 39). This twofold character is reflected in the two liturgical stages in Advent, each having its own Preface expressing its special focus.

From the First Sunday of Advent until 16 December, the liturgy expresses our hope in, and our expectation of, the coming of Christ in glory. We watch and wait for the time 'when the salvation promised us will be ours' and when 'Christ our Lord will come again in his glory' (Advent Preface I). But liturgy can only celebrate remembered historical events, memorials of God's action in history, not events yet to be. So, characteristically, the liturgical texts in this first part of Advent draw upon Isaiah and the other prophets of the Old Testament, reminding us how the human race, especially the chosen people, were prepared for Christ's first coming. These two comings of Christ are not isolated from each other. Christ's birth was the beginning of his messianic kingdom, which will reach completion when he comes in glory.

The second phase of Advent is from 17 December until Christmas Eve. The liturgical texts focus more directly upon the circumstances of Christ's coming at Bethlehem and so prepare our minds and hearts to celebrate 'his birth ... our hearts filled with wonder and praise' (Advent Preface II). This is a most poetic and eloquent period when prayers, Scripture readings and Preface II combine to express our longing for the saviour, using a mosaic of Scripture texts. The gospel acclamations of these final days of Advent are versions of the Magnificat antiphons from Evening Prayer which are called the Great 'O' antiphons. Each portrays the Messiah and the work he will accomplish. They begin in eternity, addressing Christ as 'Eternal Wisdom', and as the days progress, these acclamations span the whole of salvation history until God himself is with us: Emmanuel, to teach, enlighten, liberate and redeem us.

However, careful scrutiny of the liturgical texts reveals that the Advent liturgies interweave references to *three* comings of Christ:

> his coming in *history* as man at the incarnation;
> his coming in *majesty* at the end of time;
> his coming in *mystery* in the sacraments ...

We are living between two historical events: Christ's coming in the flesh and his coming in the future. During this interim period, Christ comes to us in his mysteries, especially in his Paschal Mystery. Advent's 'devout and joyful expectation' (GNLYC 39) is not nostalgic, nor is it 'make-believe'. The risen Christ is not bound by time and has promised to be with us until the end of time. We welcome him particularly in his sacraments, when he comes to us *today*.

Advent is not a penitential season *per se*. Nevertheless, in responding to the call of the prophets in its readings, we engage ourselves in ongoing conversion, 'as we wait in joyful hope for the coming of our Saviour, Jesus Christ' (Titus 2:13). Violet vestments are not to express penitence, but more a state of unfulfilled readiness and to provide a contrast when Christmas comes. Likewise, the omission of the Gloria is so that the hymn of the angels may resound with greater freshness on Christmas night.

The focus of each Advent Sunday remains the same for all three years of the Lectionary. The First Sunday of Advent is concerned with the Second Coming of the Lord in glory; the Second Sunday focuses on John the Baptizer calling us to conversion; the Third Sunday expresses the relationship of John and Jesus; and the Fourth relates the events that immediately preceded the birth of Jesus, especially the Annunciation to Mary and the Visitation.

A major liturgical problem is how to maintain and celebrate Advent as a *preparatory season* and not anticipate Christmas. Tension exists between the demands of the commercial world's Christmas and our Christian celebration. The commercial Christmas begins in the autumn and daily proclaims 'X number of shopping days to Christmas'. This commercial celebration ends on Christmas Eve when the shops close and when Christians are just beginning to celebrate the incarnation. The social calendar, too, can involve celebrations of Christmas before-hand in school and office parties. Letting Advent be Advent is a major challenge. Popular devotions should be consistent with the themes of the Advent Masses. Songs and carols focusing on the nativity itself are out of place in Advent, especially before 17 December. Advent carols, vigils and services of light bring out the major symbolism of the season, the coming of light out of darkness, and help to sustain watchfulness and expectancy leading to a fuller celebration of Christmas when it comes. Perhaps Christians prepare most perfectly to welcome Christ in his glory by welcoming him today in the least of his brethren – which is basically the lesson of Advent/Christmastide.

CHRISTMASTIME extends from Evening Prayer I of Christmas on 24 December, until the Sunday after Epiphany, the feast of the Baptism of the Lord. 'Next to the yearly celebration of the paschal mystery, the Church holds most sacred the memorial of Christ's birth and early manifestations. This is the purpose of the Christmas season' (GNLYC 32). Christmas is not a feast of nostalgia, but a celebration of the incarnation *today*. The liturgical texts make it abundantly clear that the Word of God became man so that we might share in his divinity (cf. Philippians 2). This word *hodie*, 'today', is the key to understanding this season. The psalm refrain for Midnight Mass proclaims: 'Today a saviour has been born to us; he is Christ the Lord' and Preface II of Christmas sings: 'Today you fill our hearts with joy as we recognise in Christ the revelation of your love.'

Much remains uncertain about the origins of the feast of Christmas, but we do know that the birth of our saviour was celebrated in Rome on 25 December in AD 336. Three theories are put forward to account for the choice of this date. First, that it was a deliberate attempt to replace the pagan feast of the unconquered Sun god on this date, by a feast celebrating Christ as the true, victorious *sol justitiae* – sun of justice. This feast closely followed the winter solstice. Secondly, early Christians tried to calculate Christ's date of birth from scriptural data. Zechariah received the promise of John the Baptist's conception when fulfilling his priestly duties at Yom Kippur. This places the conception of John in September and his birth in June (24). At the Annunciation, Mary was told that Elizabeth was 'in her sixth month' (Luke 1:36). This gives March for the conception of Jesus and 25 December for his birth. After the summer solstice the sun declines in our skies; after the winter solstice, the sun begins to increase. People linked this solar fact with the words of John: 'he must increase; I must decrease' (John 3:30). Thirdly, a considerable symbolism was recognized in celebrating our saviour's birth just after the winter solstice when the sun begins once again to conquer the darkness. Here is a visible sign of Christ's Paschal victory over the darkness of sin and death, so that we might live as a new creation. Whatever the original reasons for the choice of dates for celebrating the Nativity and Epiphany, these feasts have become filled with cosmic and solar symbolism.

Liturgically, Christmas Day is very exceptional in being provided with four separate Mass formulas in our Roman Rite: a Vigil Mass, a Mass at Midnight, a Dawn Mass and a Day Mass. This structure developed in sixth-century Rome in the following way. Originally the feast was celebrated with one daytime Mass. Then a replica of the crib at Bethlehem was built near St Mary Major and the people asked to have a nocturnal Mass as was done at Bethlehem. Before 25 December was observed as the feast of the Nativity, it was the feast of St Anastasia and was celebrated in her basilica in the Byzantine quarter of Rome. To honour these Eastern Christians, Popes began to visit her basilica on their way from the Night Mass to the Day Mass. So developed the

Dawn Mass. When the practice of celebrating these Masses developed elsewhere in Christendom (where there was no crib replica or basilica of St Anastasia), the Mass texts took on images appropriate to the sun's position in its passage from night into day. Hence these Masses of Christmas Day are seen as following the sun: at its setting, its lowest point, its rising and at full noon. So Christmas is pre-eminently a feast of *light*. 'Father, you make this night radiant with the splendour of Jesus Christ our light. We welcome him as Lord, the true light of the world' (Opening prayer, Midnight Mass).

Like Easter, Christmas has an octave, a liturgical week of feasts. Unlike Easter, these days are often saints' feasts, some presumably already fixed before the choice of 25 December as the Nativity feast. Although St Stephen (26) and St John, Apostle and Evangelist (27), had no original connection with Christmas, they have long been seen, together with the Holy Innocents (28), as the cortège of honour to accompany the infant king into the world. Each portrays a type of commitment needed to establish the kingdom of God on earth. The martyrs shed their blood in imitation of Christ; John spread the good news of salvation.

Christmas is a season, not just a day, and it contains a series of great festivals: Christmas Day itself and then its octave day, 1 January, Solemnity of Mary, Mother of God. This feast recognizes the importance of Mary's role in salvation history. The entry antiphon expresses this: 'Hail, Holy Mother! The child to whom you gave birth is the King of heaven and earth forever.' The gospel includes the giving of the name of Jesus at his circumcision, drawing attention once again to the purpose of his coming to shed his blood for us in the Paschal Mystery. His very name means 'Yahweh saves'. Christ entered our world not because he wanted to live with us, but because he wants us to live with him. As Christmas Preface II says:

> Christ is your Son before all ages,
> yet now he is born in time.
> He has come to lift up all things to himself,
> to restore unity to creation,
> and to lead us from exile into your heavenly kingdom.

The third great festival is the Epiphany, the liturgical celebration of the manifestation of Christ. This was the original feast of the Nativity in the Eastern Church. The Eastern Church was less concerned about celebrating historical events and much more concerned with celebrating the *significance* of the appearance of God in and to the world. They celebrated all the following ideas in the one feast of Epiphany or

Manifestation: the incarnation, the adoration of the Magi, the baptism of Jesus and the miracle of Cana. Over the centuries the last three mysteries have been part of this holy day. Today, the star leads the magi to the infant Christ: today, the water is changed into wine for the wedding feast: today, Christ wills to be baptized by John in the Jordan to bring us salvation (see Morning Prayer and Evening Prayer II antiphons for the Benedictus and Magnificat).

Epiphany is the original feast of Christ as king, as the opening antiphon clearly states: 'The Lord and ruler is coming; kingship is his, and government and power.' It is also celebrating the Paschal Mystery of our salvation, as the Epiphany Preface says:

> Today you revealed in Christ
> your eternal plan of salvation
> And showed him as the light of all peoples.
> Now that his glory has shone among us
> you have renewed humanity in his immortal image.

So, with Epiphany, we are once more back with the image of the Christmas season as a feast of light.

The Baptism of the Lord closes the Christmas season. This event manifested the fact that salvation is for the whole world. At his baptism, Jesus is proclaimed Son of God and anointed by the Holy Spirit. It marks the beginning of his public mission and ministry. Jesus came as the servant son, empowered by the Spirit to bring the Father's plan of salvation to completion. The voice from the cloud urges us to listen to Christ as we enter upon Ordinary Time.

Ordinary Time

Ordinary Time includes thirty-three or thirty-four weeks separated by the Lent/Eastertime season. Winter Ordinary Time lasts from the Monday after the Baptism of the Lord until Shrove Tuesday inclusive. The larger section of Ordinary Time lasts from the Monday after Pentecost until the Saturday before the First Sunday of Advent.

Although the name 'Ordinary' Time actually comes from 'ordinal' and means counted time, i.e. the weeks are numbered, the name can still be seen as symbolic and containing a message. Every life has its peak moments, but uneventful, humdrum, ordinary time composes most of our existence. Our memories and hopes focus on the mountaintop experiences but, like Jesus, we dwell in the valleys and on the plains. The gospels highlight the public ministry of Jesus, but most of his life was lived in ordinary time. We need ordinary time in order to appreciate the seasons, but it is in these lowlands of ordinary time that our lives are to bear fruit in mission and ministry for the kingdom.

From a mountain peak, the lowlands appear uniformly flat, but from the plain one sees the hills which interrupt the flatness. Special days form such 'hilltops' in the Church's Ordinary Time. The most important and regular of these is the Lord's Day, Sunday, the weekly feast day (see p. 66 above). The remaining hills are provided by some solemnities of the Lord which occur in Ordinary Time, and by the Sanctoral Cycle.

The Solemnities of the Lord which occur on weekdays are the Annunciation of the Lord (25 March); the Body and Blood of Christ (Second Thursday after Pentecost) and the Sacred Heart (Third Friday after Pentecost). These solemn festival days are specific reminders of the central mystery we celebrate, the Paschal Mystery. The Preface of the Sacred Heart, for example, proclaims:

> Lifted high on the cross,
> Christ gave his life for us,
> so much did he love us.
> From his wounded side flowed blood and water,
> the fountain of sacramental life in the Church.
> To his open heart the Saviour invites all men,
> to draw water in joy from the springs of salvation.

The Sundays of Ordinary Time are strongly influenced by the synoptic evangelists, each in turn through the three-year cycle. *Matthew* presents Jesus as rabbi, and presents the words of Jesus in five main discourses around which he weaves the rest of the narrative. His is an ecclesial gospel, concerned with the mystery of the Church and God's abiding presence with us as Emmanuel. Christ is the Messiah, the new Moses who will lead his people to freedom. *Mark*'s gospel confronts us with the person of Jesus: Son of God and Son of Man, the Messiah. The crisis point in his gospel is the question 'Who do you say that I am?' (8:29). Up to this point, Mark is progressively revealing that Jesus is the Messiah. From this point onwards, Jesus teaches that the Messiah must suffer. *Luke*, writing for Gentiles, emphasizes that Jesus is Saviour of the whole world. It is a gospel stressing the renunciation needed to follow Christ; but it is also a gospel of forgiveness and mercy for the poor, the lost and the insignificant. As followers of Jesus, his journey to the cross and to glory is our itinerary, too, and we follow him as a community of disciples.

The Sanctoral Cycle

Other hills on the green lowland of Ordinary Time are provided by the feast days of Our Lady and the saints. These 'proclaim the wonderful works of Christ in his servants and display to the faithful fitting examples for their imitation' (SC 104). These feasts occur on fixed dates in the civil calendar and are classified as solemnities, feasts and memorials. This nomenclature reminds us that some saints are important for the universal Church; others, of more local importance, may figure only on national calendars in dioceses where they have significance.

Marian feasts

From the beginning, the Church has appreciated the crucial role of Mary in the work of redemption and established feasts in her honour through the centuries. In the early Church, the main commemoration of Mary was at Christmas. Many of her feasts originated in the Eastern Church, especially after the Council of Ephesus (431) which affirmed her as Theotokos, the Mother of God. Later, the Western Church adopted these feasts. The major ones, of course, were related to those of Christ, and a cycle of Marian feasts developed parallel to the events in Christ's life. So the feast of his conception, the Annunciation (25 March), was paralleled by the Immaculate Conception (8 December); the feast of his Nativity (25 December), by the Birthday of Mary (8 September); and his Ascension by her Assumption (15 August). In the revised calendar, three Marian feasts are solemnities: the Immaculate Conception (8 December), Mary, Mother of God (1 January), and the Assumption (15 August).

The feast of the Immaculate Conception celebrates not only the full effects of the Paschal Mystery in Mary, who was preserved from sin in view of her role in redemption, but also her role as model of the Church. As always, the Preface expresses our belief:

> You allowed no stain of Adam's sin
> to touch the Virgin Mary.
> Full of grace, she was to be a worthy mother of your Son,
> your sign of favour to the Church at its beginning,
> and the promise of its perfection as the bride of Christ ...

The solemnity of Mary, Mother of God focuses on her role in salvation history in bringing Christ our saviour into the world. She is the glorious mother, seat of wisdom, presenting the redeemer to all nations. She is also our pattern of response to the Father. We, too, have to bring forth Christ to our world today.

The Assumption celebrates the fulfilment of the Paschal Mystery in Mary's death and her assumption into heavenly glory – pattern of our Christian life and sign of hope:

Today the virgin Mother of God was taken up into heaven
to be the beginning and the pattern of the Church in its perfection,
and a sign of hope and comfort for your people on their pilgrim way.
You would not allow decay to touch her body,
for she had given birth to your Son, the Lord of all life,
in the glory of the incarnation. (Preface)

Feasts of the saints

Celebrating the saints is a concrete way of showing our belief in the communion of saints. At every Mass, we join our prayers with theirs in a single community of prayer and praise. We also honour the saints as examples of Christian living.

The history of the cult of the saints is extremely complex but, in general terms, it began in the second century with local veneration of martyrs, usually at their burial place and on the anniversary of their death. To die a martyr was seen as the fullest way of sharing in Christ's Paschal Mystery and also a manifestation of that mystery in the life of the Church. The apostles, as the officially-appointed witnesses, were also venerated at this time. Later on, other forms of witnessing to Christ were added, such as confessors, monks and virgins. Historically, saints were associated with particular places.

In the course of the centuries, cult of the saints became excessive and overloaded the liturgical calendar to the detriment of the Lord's Day and the seasons. The Vatican II revision of the calendar not only involved pruning away obscure or somewhat legendary saints, but also an attempt to add names to the calendar so that every nation and age were represented.

It is neither possible nor desirable to celebrate every saint's day! Some are undoubtedly of universal significance, especially those mentioned in the New Testament. The Birth of St John the Baptist (24 June), St Joseph, Husband of Mary (19 March) and Sts Peter and Paul (29 June) are all solemnities, the highest category of saints' days. All the other apostles and evangelists are celebrated as feasts. Most saints' days are memorials, and not all of these are obligatory. Selection is essential. In line with tradition, it seems preferable to celebrate the local saints who are significant for an area, rather than more obscure figures.

Since the ninth century, the Roman Rite has celebrated a feast of All Saints (1 November) on which we honour the many named and unnamed Christians who have followed Christ in his Paschal Mystery and returned with him to the Father. As always the key image of this day is to be found in the Preface:

> Today we keep the festival of your holy city,
> the heavenly Jerusalem, our mother.
> Around your throne
> the saints, our brothers and sisters,
> sing your praise for ever.
> Their glory fills us with joy,
> and their communion with us in your Church
> gives us inspiration and strength
> as we hasten on our pilgrimage of faith,
> eager to meet them.

Keeping the liturgical and devotional memory of saints can sharpen our own longing for the heavenly Jerusalem and help us to make the Paschal Mystery of Jesus a reality in our lives.

3. Planning

To make the most of the liturgical year in a parish it is essential to develop a liturgy team to plan the year as a whole, distribute events on days which have appropriate readings and avoid overload. Sacramental liturgies such as penitential services, communal anointings of the sick, RCIA liturgies, children's first sacraments and similar, need to be carefully scheduled to avoid clashes. Detailed planning should be done for a whole season at a time, not piecemeal, Sunday by Sunday. Essential aids to such planning are an annual chart of the liturgical year, which should be posted where everyone can consult it, and the almanac of parish liturgy, *Sourcebook for Sundays and Seasons* (Chicago: Liturgy Training Publications). This not only gives guidance to parish liturgy teams, but gives ideas and makes suggestions for celebrating the liturgical year at home.

DOCUMENTATION AND BIBLIOGRAPHY

Constitution on the Liturgy, ch. 5.
General Norms for the Liturgical Year and the Calendar, included in ICEL (ed.), *Documents on the Liturgy 1963–1979* (Collegeville, MN: The Liturgical Press, 1982).

A. G. Martimort (ed.), *The Church at Prayer*, vol. IV (London: Geoffrey Chapman, 1986).

M. Searle (ed.), *Sunday Morning: A Time for Worship* (Collegeville, MN: The Liturgical Press, 1982).

United States Catholic Conference, *The Roman Calendar: Text and Commentary* (Washington, DC: USCC Publications Office, 1976).

Unit 5

PETER GALLACHER

CHRISTIAN INITIATION

> In the sacraments of Christian initiation we are freed from the power of darkness and joined to Christ's death, burial, and resurrection. We receive the Spirit of filial adoption and are part of the entire people of God in the celebration of the Lord's death and resurrection. (RCIA, General Introduction, 1)

1. History

New Testament

While the structure of Christian initiation, in the sense of God's gift of redemption and salvation coming through Christ in the Holy Spirit, is clearly visible in the New Testament, it is not possible to find there any developed ritual detail of that structure. However, the New Testament does indicate that Christian baptism has the water bath as its central ritual action; it is clear too that baptism is not in water only but also involves the giving of the Spirit. It is quite specific regarding the baptism of adults but not that of children, though it does not deny this possibility since several passages speak of an entire household being converted. Where this is so, however, it is a result of a mature faith response made by the adults of that household. Baptism is always preceded by a proclamation of the *kerygma*. Preparation also included catechesis in the mystery of Christ. Throughout the New Testament initiation is seen as crucially linked to conversion.

Developing a process and structure (second–third centuries)

During the second and third centuries we have the first written descriptions of the structure of Christian initiation. This reflects a developing pattern which eventually became a fairly well structured process. One of the first testimonies comes from the *Didache* (later first or early second century), which indicates that baptism is only to be given after a definite form of instruction. The candidates will be baptized in running water and baptism is given in the name of Father, Son and Holy Spirit. Prior to baptism the candidates are to fast and it is suggested that other members of the community could join them in this.

Justin Martyr in his *First Apology (c.* 150) provides a description of the life and worship of Christians, telling how preparation for baptism is the responsibility of both the candidates and the local church. The candidates had to display a response of faith and show that they were prepared to live according to the gospel. The community was called to support them through a period of fasting for the forgiveness of their sins.

At the beginning of the third century, the Roman priest Hippolytus in his *Apostolic Tradition* lays out in some detail the pattern and structure for Christian initiation already well established in the church of Rome. Prior to admission into the catechumenate, candidates were examined on their state and way of life and on their crafts and professions; certain activities were regarded as incompatible with the desire to lead the Christian life, and there had to be someone to testify to the candidate's suitability. The catechumenate lasted three years, though seriousness of purpose was regarded as more important than time.

The formation of the catechumens involved instruction with the rest of the community as well as individual prayer. They were not permitted to give the kiss of peace. The sessions ended with the laying-on of hands over the catechumens, prayer and dismissal.

After three years they were further examined as to whether they had lived in a way in keeping with their desire for baptism. If this was so and their sponsors spoke up on their behalf they became the 'chosen' and entered the final intense stage. The immediate preparation for sacramental initiation involved fasting and exorcisms.

During the Easter Vigil (although this is not stated specifically) baptism was celebrated towards dawn, with the children baptized first, then the men and, finally, the women. Then they were anointed with perfumed oil and brought in to the assembly; the bishop anointed them with the 'oil of thanksgiving', they prayed with the community and shared in the eucharist for the first time. The process did not come to an end with the sacraments of initiation; the newly baptized were exhorted to do good works, to devote themselves to the Church and to advance in the service of God.

The pattern outlined by Hippolytus provides the basic structure for the process of Christian initiation even today.

Beginnings of decline (fourth–fifth centuries)

By the time of the conversion of Constantine, the Church had already started to become a Church of the masses. With the Edict of Milan (AD 313), the increase in numbers became a flood and as the quantity of those seeking membership increased, the quality tended to decrease. Becoming a Christian was seen in terms of social advantage or even as a means of gaining employment. People might be enrolled in the catechumenate without any instruction or preparation. Baptism tended to be postponed until late in life because of the dire penalties for serious sin committed after baptism. The period of preparation for Easter became much more intense; Lent developed to compensate for the loss of the catechumenate. Each year, the bishop would exhort the catechumens to present themselves for baptism that Easter. Those who did so came before the bishop on the First Sunday of Lent. The *scrutinies* were celebrated on the Third, Fourth and Fifth Sundays; these were designed to purify the hearts and minds of the candidates and to affirm and strengthen what was good in their lives. The *traditiones*, the handing over of the Creed and the Lord's Prayer, were introduced into the weekdays of Lent.

Despite these attempts, reflected in the rich seam of patristic writing about Lent and the time of mystagogy (the period of post-baptismal instruction), the decline had begun.

From decline to disintegration (sixth century– Middle Ages)

By the seventh and eighth centuries, the vast majority of those to be baptized were infants. The rites of initiation were still celebrated in one ceremony, normally at the Easter Vigil, with the infants being baptized, confirmed and given the eucharist (by receiving a drop of precious blood from the finger of the priest).

Obviously any preparation of the candidates was out of the question and Lent gradually lost its intrinsic connection with initiation. The only vestiges which remained were the scrutinies which had doubled in number and which took place on a weekday rather than a Sunday. This had the unfortunate effect of weakening the Lenten Sunday Lectionary.

Until the twelfth century the celebration of the sacraments of initiation remained stable, with baptism, confirmation and eucharist celebrated together in one rite. Several factors conspired to ensure that they became separated. While baptism was still celebrated at the Easter Vigil or at Pentecost, it remained normal procedure to confirm and give the eucharist to the child. However, as churches multiplied and the bishop could not be present at every celebration of initiation, the

Roman Church reserved to the bishop the role of minister of confirmation. This would take place within a year or so of the child's birth.

During the later Middle Ages, with a sharp decline in lay communion, there was an unease about communicating infants immediately after baptism, especially as adults were no longer allowed to receive communion from the chalice. The climate of nervousness led to a move to delay the reception of communion until the age of reason, and this was enshrined in legislation by the Fourth Lateran Council in 1215.

The high rate of infant mortality during the Middle Ages, and the fear that those who died without baptism would go to hell, led parents to seek baptism for their children as soon as possible after birth. This lessened any remaining connection between baptism and the Easter Vigil and baptism was eventually celebrated on any day without distinction.

It has to be remembered, moreover, that the rites used had been designed for adults and their application to children was anything but suitable.

Moves to restoration and renewal

In our own century, progress in patristic studies has led to fresh interest in the great initiatory and mystagogical homilies of the Fathers, and this in turn to a deeper appreciation of the original structure of Christian initiation. Following the restoration of the Easter Vigil to its correct time, there came a growth in awareness of the connection between baptism and Easter. Coupled with this, some parts of Europe, most notably France, saw a significant decline in the number of children baptized. The need to respond to this new situation led to a strong desire for a restored catechumenate adapted for contemporary situations.

The catechumenate restored – Vatican II

In 1962, on the eve of the Council, the Sacred Congregation of Rites moved with surprising haste to publish a decree restoring the rite of baptism of adults in stages. This was supposed to be in keeping with the early tradition of the Church and the catechumenate, but the texts used were simply those of the old ritual with the rite divided into seven parts. Nothing had really changed, least of all the spirit of the rite. This made the need for a true restoration of the catechumenate all the more pressing.

In the documents of Vatican II, the notion of Christian initiation emerged in a clear way. *Ad Gentes*, the Council document on the

Church's missionary activity, describes the sacraments of Christian initiation as follows:

> Then, when the sacraments of Christian Initiation have freed them from the power of darkness (cf. Colossians 1:13), having died with Christ, been buried with him, and risen with him they receive the Spirit who makes them adopted sons, and celebrate the remembrance of the Lord's death and resurrection together with the whole People of God. (14)

It goes on to underline that the whole Church has a part to play in the work of initiation:

> This Christian Initiation, which takes place during the catechumenate, should not be left entirely to the priests and catechists, but should be the concern of the whole Christian community, especially of the sponsors, so that from the beginning the catechumens will feel that they belong to the people of God.

A further clarification emerges regarding the relationship of initiation and the liturgical year:

> It is desirable that the Liturgy of Lent and Paschal time should be restored in such a way that it will serve to prepare the hearts of the catechumens for the celebration of the Paschal Mystery, at whose solemn ceremonies they are reborn to Christ in Baptism.

The Constitution on the Sacred Liturgy, which appeared earlier, is less well developed. However, it does call for a restoration of the catechumenate:

> The catechumenate for adults, comprising several distinct steps, is to be restored and brought into use at the discretion of the local ordinary. By this means the time of the catechumenate, which is intended as a period of suitable instruction, may be sanctified by sacred rites to be celebrated at successive intervals of time (64)

In calling for the introduction of a rite of infant baptism and the revision of the rite of confirmation, Vatican II was stressing the unity of the sacraments of initiation:

The rite of confirmation is to be revised so that the intimate connection of this sacrament with the whole of Christian Initiation may more clearly appear. (SC 71)

The concrete results of the recommendations of the Council came with the publication of the *Ordo Baptismi Parvulorum* (1969), *Ordo Confirmationis* (1971) and, finally, *Ordo Initiationis Christianae Adultorum* (1972). After many years of an interim text the officially approved version for the Dioceses of England and Wales and Scotland, the *Rite of Christian Initiation of Adults*, appeared in 1987. In terms of its length and importance, the RCIA was second only to the *Ordo Missae*. In terms of its vision and potential impact on the Church, it is perhaps the most important of the post-Vatican II liturgies.

2. The spirit and vision of RCIA

RCIA does not exist in a vacuum. It requires a parish imbued with the spirit of the rites which has a genuine and apparent desire to welcome new members. Catholics sometimes assume that the Church is seen as always ready to welcome new members, but this is often far from how things are viewed from outside.

RCIA shows a Church which has moved away from a privatized view of 'becoming a convert' towards a recognition that many people have a role to play in welcoming new members. Instead of a set series of talks on the Church's belief and practice, the journey is centred on the process of conversion. Rather than the course of private instruction involving a few individuals, the process involves the contribution of many and must be an essential part of parish life. Formerly, 'convert classes' could take place at any time, the aim being to complete the course as quickly as possible. RCIA is integral to the liturgical year, with the climax of the journey at the Easter Vigil. To respect the spirit of the rites, it is of vital importance to view the faith journey of the individual and conversion to Christ as the controlling factors rather than any preoccupation with time. Adaptation is an essential feature of RCIA.

Therefore, in no sense can the RCIA be viewed as a 'recipe book'. In fact it cannot begin to be used until those involved in implementing it have been imbued with a real sense of a Church which treasures the input, initiatives and gifts of many. The richness of the rites cannot be discovered simply by reading the book, though the Introduction or *Praenotanda* gives a marvellous synthesis of the living theology which permeates the rites, particularly the central fact that it is a process with steps and stages. Reality and life are easier to cope with when split up into manageable parts.

RCIA: steps and stages

The following are the steps and stages in the RCIA. The sections in *italic* come from the overview of the rites given in the RCIA book, page 14.

Period of evangelization and pre-catechumenate

This is a time of no fixed duration or structure, for inquiry and introduction to gospel values, an opportunity for the beginnings of faith.

This is a time for asking questions. It is important for the *enquirers* to ask the questions, rather than have them decided in advance. It is a time for introductions, when the enquirers meet members of the parish informally. It is also a part of the work of evangelization and continues what has already taken place in order to bring people to this stage.

The pre-catechumenate is also the time to ascertain the enquirer's situation. Certain difficulties may present themselves and it is as well to be aware of them sooner rather than later.

Care must be taken not to force or pressurize or to assume that this stage is any more than an enquiry made in good will. The enquirer may decide not to go any further or may want to postpone a decision, and those involved in the pre-catechumenate should not feel they have failed if this happens.

For the *enquirers* this is a time when, recognizing the presence of God in their lives, they are helped to listen to God's invitation to respond to his love by following his Son, Jesus, and to decide whether this response involves becoming a member of the Catholic Church.

First Step: acceptance into the Order of Catechumens

This is the liturgical rite, usually celebrated on some annual date or dates, marking the beginning of the catechumenate proper, as the candidates express and the church accepts their intention to respond to God's call to follow the way of Christ.

The decision to become a catechumen is taken by both the enquirer and the parish, but primarily by the enquirer. After a time spent finding out about the Church in the context of a continuing journey of faith, this decision marks a significant step towards initiation into the Church. In the celebration of this liturgy enquirers assemble publicly for the first time. As with all the liturgies of RCIA, the community should show its support by its presence (RCIA 45), particularly those who have been chosen as sponsors for the new catechumens. There is no set date for the Rite of Acceptance and it may be celebrated several times a year depending on circumstances.

The catechumenate

This is the time, in duration corresponding to the progress of the individual, for the nurturing and growth of the catechumens' faith and conversion to God; celebrations of the word and prayers of exorcism and blessing are meant to assist the process.

The catechumenate is a time for the catechumens to grow in faith and joyfully discover the presence of God in their lives. It does not last for a fixed period; it is important to allow as much time as necessary. The catechumenate normally has two complementary dimensions. There is the breaking open of the Word following the Liturgy of the Word at Sunday Mass, and also a weekly gathering of catechists, catechumens, sponsors and others, the purpose of which is the ongoing conversion of the catechumens and their formation in the faith. There is no 'textbook' for these sessions other than the Lectionary, but they should cover the essentials of Catholic faith and practice. The RCIA sums up this stage as follows:

> The instruction that the catechumens receive during this period
> should be of a kind that while presenting Catholic faith in its
> entirety also enlightens faith, directs the heart towards God,
> fosters participation in the liturgy, inspires apostolic activity,
> and nurtures a life completely in accord with the spirit of Christ.

Second Step: election or enrolment of names

This is the liturgical rite, usually celebrated on the First Sunday of Lent, by which the Church formally ratifies the catechumens' readiness for the sacraments of initiation and the catechumens, now the elect, express the will to receive these sacraments.

If this liturgy is to be celebrated in an authentic way, real discernment of the candidates' readiness must have taken place. The responsibility for this rests with the parish. Through the sponsors and others crucially involved in the catechumens' journey, and after a dialogue with the catechumens themselves, they are chosen by the parish and become the 'elect' when the bishop ratifies the decision during the Rite of Election. This liturgy, which normally takes place in the cathedral, also allows the candidates themselves to realize that the Church is much wider than the parish.

Adaptation is a keyword of RCIA, and already this part of the rites has been much adapted. Many parishes have drawn up their own rite of 'sending' the catechumens to the cathedral. The rite of election has also been adapted to take account of the fact that some of those involved in the process are already baptized.

Period of purification and enlightenment

This is the time immediately preceding the initiation of the elect, usually the Lenten season preceding the celebration of this initiation at the Easter Vigil; it is a time of reflection, intensely centred on conversion, marked by celebration of the scrutinies and presentations and of the preparation rites on Holy Saturday.

The influence of initiation on Lent can happily be seen once again. The *General Norms for the Liturgical Year* state that 'the liturgy prepares the catechumens for the celebration of the paschal mystery by the several stages of Christian Initiation' (27). Lent can only be fully understood within the context of initiation. The Lenten Lectionary of Year A, always to be used where there are candidates for baptism, uses the great Johannine texts of the Samaritan woman at the well (thirst for living water), the man born blind (darkness to light) and the raising of Lazarus (death to life) on the Third, Fourth and Fifth Sundays, the days when the scrutinies are celebrated. These are to 'uncover, then heal all that is weak, defective or sinful in the hearts of the elect' and to 'bring out, then strengthen all that is upright, strong and good' (RCIA 28). Lent is also the time for the *presentations*, the handing over of the Creed and the Lord's Prayer.

Third Step: celebration of the sacraments of initiation

This is the liturgical rite, usually integrated into the Easter Vigil, by which the elect are initiated through baptism, confirmation, and the eucharist.

The climax of the journey takes place at the climax of the liturgical year. There is insufficient space here for a detailed examination of the Vigil liturgy. Briefly, however, the baptismal part of the Vigil has the following outline.

THE CALLING OF THE CANDIDATES

Those who are to be baptized, and their godparents, are called to the font. There is no need for rehearsals with the elect; what is about to happen is new and should be experienced as such. Those who are presiding and/or exercising other ministries, however, should be well prepared. For the sake of those approaching baptism the liturgy must flow smoothly.

LITANY OF THE SAINTS

Litanies are for singing. The names of those to be baptized, the patrons of the parish and other saints may be added to those in the Rite; litanies glory in repetition and lose their character if abbreviated.

BLESSING OF THE WATER

RENUNCIATION OF SIN AND PROFESSION OF FAITH

The renunciation is done by questioning each individual or the group together, according to the number of candidates. The Profession of Faith is made individually, unless numbers make this difficult. Each candidate is baptized immediately following his or her profession of faith.

BAPTISM

The Church has a clear preference for baptism by immersion over the pouring of water. Establishing this as normal policy is a challenge, but once established it will be easier to maintain it as the norm. Among the details to be settled (well in advance of the Vigil) are the clothes to be worn, the facilities for changing, the adaptation of the existing font, etc. After each Baptism a brief acclamation may be sung.

EXPLANATORY RITES

CLOTHING WITH A WHITE GARMENT

This (optional) rite reinforces symbolically what has just taken place in the waters of baptism. Local custom will decide an appropriate form for the white garment; the alb is the robe of the baptized, but this could be misconstrued as involving some clericalization of the person.

PRESENTATION OF THE LIGHTED CANDLE

The candle is lit from the Paschal candle and given to the newly baptized by their godparents. The presider adds his words of encouragement and the newly baptized respond 'Amen'.

(*If there are candidates for full communion then the Renewal of Baptismal Promises takes place now followed by the celebration of Reception.*)

CELEBRATION OF CONFIRMATION

This ceremony, seen in its ideal, normative context, is simple and straightforward. Conferred by the laying-on of hands over the group and the individual anointing with chrism, the gift of the Spirit in baptism is seen as deputing for worship. The greatest expression of witness to what has been gifted in initiation is made in the celebration of eucharist. The liturgy, if planned carefully, now flows naturally into the general intercessions in which the newly baptized join for the first time, and the entire vigil moves towards its climax in the Liturgy of the Eucharist.

Period of post-baptismal catechesis or mystagogy

This is the time, usually the Easter season, following the celebration of initiation, during which the newly initiated experience being fully a part of the Christian community by means of both pertinent catechesis and particularly by participation with all the faithful in the Sunday eucharistic celebration.

As Lent is given its full significance by the presence of the elect and their journey towards initiation, so the Easter season takes on a richer dimension if the parish is able to rejoice with the newly baptized as they are fed at the Lord's table in the eucharists of Eastertide.

The support offered by the parish through the RCIA team, and the dynamism established during the catechumenate, should continue after Easter. If it suddenly disappears, the new Christian may feel lost and bewildered. Many groups have a monthly meeting with the neophytes throughout the first year after they are baptized.

Ministry

RCIA can only operate successfully in a parish which is convinced of the need to bring a wide variety of gifts and insights to the work of sharing faith. All the ministries involved are part of the global ministry of a parish committed to sharing the good news of Jesus Christ. The introduction to the rites outlines in detail some of the ministries involved.

COMMUNITY

The entire community helps candidates through the process. Parishioners should show that this is a parish which actually wants to welcome new members; if not, there is work to be done. Their concern can be shown by their presence at the liturgies and the welcome they give to new members after their initiation (cf. RCIA 9).

SPONSOR

Appointed by the community, the sponsor is a companion on the journey and a source of encouragement. This ministry involves explaining about the activities and life of the parish and introducing the catechumens to other parishioners. The sponsor is called to witness to the progress of the candidate before the liturgical assembly (cf. RCIA 10).

GODPARENT

Normally chosen by the candidate, the godparent's ministry begins with the Rite of Election. The godparent is to be a source of support in the faith, not only in the final approach to the celebration of initiation but on a lifelong basis (cf. RCIA 11).

BISHOP

As the head of the local church, the bishop is ultimately responsible for setting up and maintaining the RCIA process in the diocese. Liturgically speaking, the bishop's role is most clearly seen in the Rite of Election, in celebrating initiation at the Easter Vigil (although this is not always feasible) and in presiding at a eucharistic celebration with the newly baptized during Eastertide.

PRIEST

The priest is responsible for the pastoral and personal care of the catechumens. He is to help especially the hesitant and those who feel discouraged. The arrangement of catechetical instruction and the correct celebration of all the rites in the course of the RCIA process also fall under his guidance.

CATECHIST

The catechist has the vitally important ministry of passing on the Church's tradition through catechesis and prayer. Catechists are also called to be aware of the candidates' own situations and to adjust their approach accordingly. This ministry is one which does not require academic teaching qualifications but, rather, an ability to share one's own faith journey in the light of God's Word. The catechist also has a liturgical role in the celebration of blessings and exorcisms during the catechumenate.

CANDIDATE

While not stated explicitly, it is obvious from the spirit of RCIA that the candidates have an important ministry towards the community. In witnessing to the God who is working in their lives and through their desire to live the faith, they call the community to examine its way of life and reflect on its own need for conversion.

RCIA CO-ORDINATOR

Once a parish embarks on RCIA it will soon be necessary to find someone to co-ordinate the different areas of activity and the ministries. It is the one role which calls for a thorough understanding of the theology and liturgy of the rites. The person chosen must be able to relate well to other people, besides having a deep personal commitment to the process.

3. The Rite of Baptism for Children

The first rite of baptism ever produced specifically for children was the *Ordo Baptismi Parvulorum* in 1969. Its arrival several years prior to RCIA has resulted, at times, in a misunderstanding as to which rite is normative for initiation. In fact the RCIA is the norm from which all the structure of Christian initiation is derived.

The Rite of Baptism for Children is rich in symbolic language and unless this is recognized it can easily become a word-dominated liturgy.

An overview of the rite: four places for this liturgy

The rite of infant baptism unfolds at four different places, which allow its 'languages' to be spoken and heard.

1. The door

The parents, godparents and children gather at the *door* of the church, a gesture which speaks of parents who present their children for baptism and a parish community eager to welcome new members into God's family.

This encounter takes place in an atmosphere of mutual joy but also recognizes the seriousness of the request being made. After listening to the parents and questioning them about their responsibilities, the parish community welcomes the children and their families. The children are marked with the sign of the cross, a gesture they will make throughout their lives as they enter the church building and when they begin and conclude the eucharist.

Within Mass, this part of the rite takes the place of the penitential rite.

2. The table of the Word

Having moved into the church, the families process to the *ambo* from which the Word of God is proclaimed.

Even when baptism is celebrated outside Mass, the place for the proclamation of the Word is one of the focal points.

3. The font

The next movement is to the baptismal *font* itself. The children are washed three times in water and baptized in the name of the Holy Trinity. All present should be able to see this rite easily.

Still at the font, four additional symbolic rites express different aspects of the event which has taken place. The children are anointed with oil, clothed in new white garments, given (through their parents and godparents) a candle lit from the Paschal candle, and touched on the ears and mouth.

4. The altar

After baptism comes a strong statement of the connection between entrance into the church through baptism and the climax of initiation in the eucharist. Initiation is incomplete until the children celebrate *confirmation* and come to the Lord's table to receive the *eucharist.*

This is highlighted through the flow of the liturgy itself when baptism takes place within Mass. Attention moves to the *altar* and the Liturgy of the Eucharist. Outside Mass there is a processional movement towards the altar. The symbolism of this should be allowed to speak for itself, rather than through a running commentary. The introduction to the Lord's Prayer does this quite effectively.

It is important for the various dialogues of the rite to be audible, by means of amplification if necessary.

Ministry in the celebration of the baptism of children

Community

The duty and privilege of welcoming new members into the Church belongs to the parish community. This cannot be stressed too highly. Some members of the parish should always be present at celebrations of baptism; it should be one of the high points of parish life, seen in the way it is celebrated.

The parish policy regarding the frequency of celebration should bear this vital principle in mind. A monthly celebration in a medium-sized parish would not seem too often. When the celebration takes place within the parish Sunday Mass then at least the physical presence of others is assured. Where baptism takes place outside Mass it may require time before parishioners feel the need for active involvement and take ownership of the work of initiation, but this should not be dismissed as an impossible dream.

Priest or deacon

The priest's role covers two areas, preparation and celebration.

The priest has to ensure that the families are prepared for the celebration and for the role of formation of their children in the faith. He should be assisted by a preparation team who will provide a programme to be followed, adaptable to the situation of each family.

The priest has to ensure that the celebration is carried out with *dignity, exactness* and *reverence*, and that it is 'as far as possible, adapted to the circumstances and wishes of the families concerned'. Finally he is to 'try to be understanding and friendly to all'. To do this, he must be familiar with the rite itself, familiar with the families, aware of the make-up of the assembly before him and open to the possibilities of adaptation and variety. This demands time to prepare and calls for the priest periodically to refresh his memory of the rite's different elements and dynamics.

Ministers of welcome

The minister of welcome gives the initial informal welcome to the families. To respect the flow and dynamic of the rite, they should not enter the church before the ceremony begins; if possible, there should be a room, close to the door of the church, where families can gather before the liturgy begins, and where the baby can be changed and fed if necessary. Families should not be kept waiting in a draughty porch.

Many people at a baptism are on unfamiliar territory, and the ministers of welcome can do much to put them at their ease. It is an opportunity for real 'outreach' whose impact cannot be overstressed.

Reader

The children's families may provide the readers, if possible. The parish readers could help by enquiring whether the family will be able to provide readers, by preparing them or by providing a reader from their own number.

The number of readers required will depend on the situation. For example, where baptism is celebrated outside of Mass, there may be more reason to have a fairly short Liturgy of the Word. (This would be so particularly in the situation where baptism immediately follows a Sunday Mass in which the families of the children have taken part.)

Musicians

When the celebration takes place within Mass, some of the parish musicians will normally be present. There is a real challenge for them to provide music for baptisms outside Mass.

The music ministers should be aware of what parts of the liturgy call for singing (see below, p. 101).

Instrumentalists and a cantor can help enormously to give warmth and a festive tone to the liturgy and their presence shows the importance the parish attaches to the celebration of all baptisms.

Servers

Servers are sometimes regarded as superfluous in the post-Vatican II liturgy, but at infant baptism servers can carry out a real ministry. They can form and lead processions, hold the book, bring items when required (e.g. oil, candles, white garment), guide the parents and god-parents, and generally help the liturgy go smoothly.

Preparation

Families must be supported and helped to prepare for their children's baptism. The ministry of preparation belongs to the priest in a special way, but is shared by the whole parish. Many parishes already have programmes of preparation in which all parents of children to be baptized must take part.

The parish liturgy group

As with every aspect of parish liturgy planning, the preparation of the celebration of infant baptism belongs to the parish liturgy group. The group may decide to devote a time – perhaps a whole year – to reviewing the way this liturgy is celebrated. The following questions are pertinent:

- How often is the sacrament celebrated in our parish? At what intervals? Do we have a policy regarding the timetabling of baptism?
- Do we respect the four different places called for in the rite (door, lectern, font, altar)?
- Do our liturgical ministers have an awareness of their roles in the celebration?
- Is there music at every parish celebration of baptism?
- Where baptism is celebrated outside Mass, do we ensure that some

parishioners are present and that a variety of liturgical roles are carried out?

- Are we moving towards making full immersion the preferred option for baptism in our parish (as in the Church's liturgical books)?
- Do we make provision for looking after young children, so that parents and godparents can take a real part in the Liturgy of the Word?
- Is our font truly worthy and dignified? Have we looked for ways in which the area surrounding the font can echo what is taking place in the water of baptism (e.g. plants, symbols, colours)?
- Is there a good level of awareness in our parish regarding the importance of the liturgy of infant baptism? If not, how can we increase that awareness?

Symbols

The community

One of the most basic symbols is the community gathered to welcome new members into the parish family. The presence and power of this symbol is of fundamental importance.

Water

The first option for baptism is immersion. This calls for a new approach to fonts; it is hardly expressive of the meaning of baptism if it takes place in something not much bigger than a salad bowl.

To celebrate a sacrament as radical as baptism, with its images of death and new birth, dying and rising with Christ, the Church employs a symbolism which urges us to go far beyond mere validity. We must give the liturgy a chance to speak and appeal to the senses, not just the intellect.

The water should be clean and warm. Ensuring this could provide the parish with a new ministry!

Interpretative symbolic rites

All that follows the baptismal bath is secondary to, and illustrative of, the primary symbol of water. However, care should be taken to let these symbols speak. The four symbolic actions are:

- anointing with chrism on the crown of the head, in silence
- putting white garments on the children
- giving and receiving a lighted candle

• touching the ears and the mouth of each child with the thumb.

Oil

This beautiful perfumed oil should be seen, and, ideally, smelt. It should be honoured by the beauty of the container in which it is held. The oil of chrism should be placed in a prominent position – perhaps on a table close to the Paschal candle – and should be used generously. It should not suddenly appear like a small jar of medical ointment, rubbed on and off before anyone knows what has happened, which risks putting forward an almost magical concept of the sacramental action.

White garment

The assumption is that the child will be naked during the baptism itself, so the clothing with the white garment forms a natural sequel to the bathing in the waters of baptism. This implies there will be a whole process of clothing, applying talc, putting on nappies and so on, which the parents and godparents will see to. The white garment should be put in a significant place until this moment.

Candle

The candle mirrors the importance of what has taken place; to pass on the light of Christ is no small responsibility and privilege. The candle should be new, substantial and perhaps decorated. It could be suggested that it might be lit each year on the anniversary of baptism (and birthdays?) and used in years to come at the renewal of baptismal promises at the Easter Vigil, at the celebration of confirmation and at other renewals of baptismal promises.

Needless to say, the Paschal candle should appear worthy and authentic. Candles which are in reality three inches high and placed on the top of a false candle do not suggest the presence of the risen Lord and have no place in Catholic liturgy.

Music

Music plays an important part in the celebration of baptism. Those involved in the ministry of music should ensure that they are thoroughly familiar with the flow of the rite and the points which call for singing. To give these in summary form, they are as follows:

At the reception of the children	*'A psalm or suitable hymn'*
Procession to the place for the Liturgy of the Word	*'A song is sung (e.g. Ps 84:7, 8, 9b)'*
Liturgy of the Word	*Responsorial Psalm* *The Gospel Acclamation*
The Litany of the Saints	
Procession to baptistery	*'An appropriate song (e.g. Ps 22)'*
After each baptism	*'It is appropriate for the people to sing a short acclamation'*
Procession to the altar	*'A baptismal song is appropriate at this time'*
After the blessing	*'All may sing a hymn which suitably expresses thanksgiving and Easter Joy, or they may sing the song of the blessed Virgin Mary, the Magnificat'*

There is a great challenge here for musicians to involve people. 'Responsorial' settings, with the assembly replying with a short response, give everyone present, even those who are not practising or Catholic, a chance to take part.

There is also a challenge to see that music is always provided in the liturgy. The first step is an agreement among all those involved that baptism is one of the most important events in parish life.

4. Confirmation

The Constitution on the Sacred Liturgy of Vatican II asked for the reform of the celebration of confirmation in the following paragraph:

> The rite of Confirmation is to be revised also so that the intimate connection of this sacrament with the whole of Christian initiation may more clearly appear. For this reason the renewal of baptismal promises should fittingly precede the reception of the sacrament. Confirmation may be conferred within Mass when convenient. For conferring outside Mass, a formula introducing the rite should be drawn up. (SC 71)

The intention here was clearly to link confirmation more closely with baptism and eucharist. After much consultation between Vatican departments, the *Ordo Confirmationis* was approved in 1971 and published by decree on 22 August 1971 in the Apostolic Constitution *Divinae Consortium Naturae*. Although the Constitution makes it clear that one of the principal aims of the revision was to bring out clearly the connection between confirmation and the whole of Christian initiation, the fact that this rite was published before the RCIA has led to continued misunderstanding. That RCIA is normative for all initiation is accepted. But when a rite of one of its components emerges prior to the normative procedure then it is not surprising that difficulties can arise.

The character of Christian initiation is clearly expressed in the outline of the rite and in the Apostolic Constitution (cf. the opening paragraph) and the order of the sacraments is clearly laid out so that confirmation is seen as the second sacrament of initiation.

Confirmation's close link with baptism is set forth ritually in the revised *Ordo Confirmationis*, in the renewal of baptismal promises and also in celebration within Mass. Formerly the celebration had no Mass texts or readings, but now a series of texts is provided.

One of the more difficult issues was to specify the essential rite of confirmation. All the earlier tradition pointed to the laying-on of hands as being the essential rite. However, the Apostolic Constitution states that the essential part is the chrismation which is by its nature a laying-on of the hand: 'The sacrament of Confirmation is conferred through the anointing with chrism on the forehead, which is done by the laying on of the hand, and through the words: *Accipe signaculum doni Spiritus Sancti.*' In attempting to define the essential rite of the sacrament, however, this declaration interferes with the integrity of the historical Roman rite. It must be said that confusion still reigns and that the Apostolic Constitution has not effectively clarified anything.

The new sacramental formula ('Be sealed with the gift of the Holy Spirit') is very similar to the corresponding formula in the Orthodox Church. The gift *is* the Spirit – it is not simply a question of the gifts of the Spirit.

The introduction to the Rite, paragraph 5, says that the sponsor who acted at baptism may again be the sponsor for confirmation, further underscoring the link between confirmation and baptism.

The question of an appropriate age for confirmation has been much discussed. The Consilium did not manage to resolve this problem; the Congregation for the Doctrine of the Faith gave episcopal conferences the authority to decide, which has led to a wide variety of approaches.

Even to ask the question may indicate an underlying attitude which sees the reception of sacraments as tied up with biological stages rather than as part of a journey in faith. Confirmation is sometimes described as a sacrament of 'growing up', maturity or adolescence – a rite of passage; but this was not the original idea, and the essence of a sacrament cannot be changed by 'modern theology'. It is a mistaken attempt to explain something which, as we have seen, resulted from an unfortunate historical accident, the separation of confirmation from the other sacraments of initiation, baptism and eucharist, with which it is necessarily bound up. Whatever age is chosen is secondary to the need to maintain the integrity and nature of the sacramental rite itself; the decision will always have to justify itself according to this criterion. The whole aim of the revision was to clarify the initiatory character of the sacrament and its intimate connection with the whole of Christian initiation. Moreover, the view of confirmation as a sacrament of adolescence rests on questionable psychological theory; delaying it until adolescence means asking for commitment when those receiving the sacrament may be approaching a low ebb in their faith.

In a parish permeated by the spirit of RCIA, both the preparation and the celebration of confirmation should be clearly seen within the unifying context of initiation.

Christian initiation today – some problems

The sequence of the sacraments

RCIA is normative, so the unity of the three sacraments of initiation is a part of that norm. In Part II of the RCIA (Rites for Particular Circumstances) the first section is entitled 'Christian Initiation of Children of a Catechetical Age'. In keeping with the spirit of the rites, this proposes a journey of faith, adapted to the situation of the children, at the end of which they are baptized, confirmed and brought to the Lord's table. As things stand this form is seldom used. Most Catholics are baptized as infants with the other two sacraments of initiation being 'received' years later; the most common pattern is first communion at the age of seven or eight and confirmation several years after that. The disruption of the recognized sequence of the sacraments is something crying out for attention and remedy. Equally important, however, is the real danger of allowing the journey of faith with its crucial conversion dimension to be overlooked or replaced by a type of catechesis or religious instruction which cannot possibly cope at this level. This difficulty is compounded where the parish has abdicated the responsibility of initiating new members and leaves this task to others who cannot be expected to take on that role.

Initiation and reconciliation

A further problem is that current legislation seems to call for the celebration of the sacrament of reconciliation for children before initiation has been completed. This makes it more difficult to experience the dynamism and shape of initiation, and the sacraments are experienced as three individual moments with no intrinsic connection.

Postponement of baptism

Parents or a single parent often request baptism for their children but give little hope that they will be brought up to practise the faith. In the Instruction on Infant Baptism (Congregation for the Doctrine of the Faith, 1980) the principle is enunciated that 'the Church must have a well-founded hope that the baptism will bear fruit'. However, it is important that the Church is seen not as *refusing* baptism but rather delaying it. The difficulty comes with trying to balance the need to avoid indiscriminate baptism with the need to give every encouragement to parents. Such situations need sensitivity, discernment and understanding.

DOCUMENTATION AND BIBLIOGRAPHY

Rite of Christian Initiation of Adults: A Study Book (London: St Thomas More Centre, 1988).

Gerald Austin, *Anointing with the Spirit* (New York: Pueblo, 1978).

J. D. Crichton, *Christian Celebration: Understanding the Sacraments* (new edn; London: Geoffrey Chapman, 1993), chs 3, 4, 5 and 6.

Aidan Kavanagh, *The Shape of Baptism: The Rite of Christian Initiation* (New York: Pueblo, 1978).

A. G. Martimort (ed.), *The Church at Prayer*, vol. III (London: Geoffrey Chapman, 1981), ch. 1.

D. A. Withey, *Catholic Worship* (Bury St Edmunds: Kevin Mayhew, 1990), ch. 10.

Unit 6

ROBIN GIBBONS OSB

CHURCH ART AND ARCHITECTURE

> When churches are to be built, let great care be taken that they be suitable for the celebration of liturgical services and for the active participation of the faithful. (SC 124)

Introduction

People are conscious that our immediate environment is crucial to our existence as human beings. Not only does it affect the way we live, but it helps create an atmosphere and ambience which touch the depths of human feeling, hopes and aspirations. Therefore in the Church's life, the environment of our worship is more than just a building with furnishings, it is a place where we celebrate our history and encounter the presence of our God with us. This is achieved through the symbols and signs of our ritual, through word, silence, song, gesture and those arts which involve the whole human experience. For these reasons, the buildings we use for worship, their architectural and artistic forms, are seen as places of communication and action, where the patterns of our lives are mirrored in the gatherings that celebrate the hopes, fears, joys and sadness of our journey in faith. The environment of our worship should be life-enhancing, uplifting, capable of leading us to that encounter with each other and the Lord which deepens our understanding of who we are as the people of God (SC 122).

Our Christian buildings have a long and varied history. Each age has used styles, materials and methods that have underpinned and consolidated the gospel lived out in that particular age of religious belief. The art and architecture of the Church has never been an optional extra, it has been rooted in a sense of place where the Christian assembly has met week by week, year by year, to nourish and strengthen its faith.

The building: *domus Dei, domus ecclesiae*

The earliest Christian community had a strong identity as a 'living building'. They described themselves as the living temple (1 Corinthians 6:19) in the midst of which God dwelt. As they grew in numbers and settled in communities, they called the buildings that housed their liturgical gatherings *domus ecclesiae*, or the house of the living Church. Though this sense of a living building (a holy people with God in their midst) was never lost, later ages assimilated other influences taken from various traditions which laid a greater stress on the physical building as a house of God. People needed a sense of belonging, of having a specific place where God could be encountered in a special way. So through history the churches took on aspects of sacredness; they were marked off by special zones of holiness and objects within them were treated wth great respect. These buildings were known as *domus Dei*, or the house of God. Today our theological understanding of church space reflects these two traditions, but it recognizes that the primary use of the building has always been to house the holy people of God and to serve its needs. However, as we are a people who feel the need to belong, it is also an identifiable building which is marked out as a special place where God will be present among his people, especially in the celebration of the eucharist and in the other liturgical gatherings that take place there.

A community needs a specific place for worship; the place is often the result of the sacrifice and generosity of individuals and communities. The Church dedicates these buildings for liturgical use and that is why the central features and furnishings contained within them have a symbolic function in helping the community celebrate and discover the abiding presence of God amongst them. The church building is a house of God and the Church. As such it needs beauty to uplift the spirit, space in which to celebrate, symbols and furnishings to engage the deeper consciousness of a people involved in their commitment to the Gospel of Christ. But above all it is a place of service where the living temple is built up by its Lord.

The presences of Christ

(a) The assembly

In the liturgical environment we encounter varying modes of the presence of Christ. Above all, the primary symbol is the gathered people in which he manifests his presence. The *assembly* is the gathered Church with its Lord. Through history this has been seen in different ways. From the earliest times, the hallmark of Christianity was the assembly gathered to celebrate the eucharist, the particularly Christian act of worship. This gathering has its roots in the gatherings called by God recorded in the Scriptures. In Christianity this assembly was open to all the baptized and led by one who presided at worship, offered prayer in the name of the community, said the thanksgiving prayer over the gifts of bread and wine and preached the Word of God. Participation was for all, though specific duties were allocated to certain categories of people: the presbyters who worked with the leader (the bishop); deacons who proclaimed the gospel, distributed the holy gifts and, with the deaconesses, catechized and looked after the temporal needs of the community; cantors who led the singing; catechists who instructed the catechumens preparing for baptism; and other ministries which developed as different needs arose.

As the Church grew in numbers, parishes were set up and the presbyter (priest) led the normal Sunday assembly in a church smaller than the bishop's cathedral. In the course of history the participation of the assembly has taken various forms; the prominence of the clergy and the separation of sanctuary and nave meant that the people have sometimes been reduced to spectators. Since the Second Vatican Council the aim of the liturgical reforms has been to restore to the people their right to a full and conscious participation in the liturgy (SC 11). In spatial terms this means that the primary requirement of our church buildings is the needs of the assembly gathered to celebrate Word and sacrament.

(b) The font

The two major sacraments of the Church have always been the rites of initiation and the eucharist. Therefore the particular focal points associated with these will be important in the planning and furnishings of a church. If the presence of Christ is seen firstly in the symbol of the gathered community, then the primary symbols of initiation and eucharist will mediate Christ's presence seen in the actions of that gathering. The *baptismal font* is a symbol of the entrance of the Christian into the death and resurrection of Christ within his body, the Church. As such it is not a vessel used only for baptisms, but a permanent symbol of the living water that gives life. The various instructions that detail the planning requirements of the liturgy suggest that a proper space be given to the font, that it should be seen by all and used as a place of gathering. It should be large enough for total immersion or, if that is impracticable, at least for partial immersion. The importance of living water cannot be overstated and in this respect great care is needed in the design and situation of the font. It is not appropriate to situate it in close proximity to the altar and the ambo.

(c) The ambo

In the eucharistic assembly we are nourished at the table of God's Word and the table of the sacrament. Christ is the living Word proclaimed from the table of the Word, the *ambo* or lectern. As this is a symbol of the place where Christ is present in the Scriptures, special attention must be given to its position and design. It is intimately linked to the assembly, who gather to hear the Word and respond to it in prayer and song. It is linked to the altar where the Word made flesh, present in the holy gifts, is broken and distributed to us in communion. It is linked to the presider who breaks the Word for all in the homily and presides over the community in the name of the Lord. It must therefore be planned with these places in mind, linked to them through design and given due honour as a place of specific importance. The crucial factor is that it should enable the assembly to participate fully and not merely spectate. Its position can be flexible and not necessarily restricted to the 'sanctuary' area.

(d) The altar

The *altar* is the main focal point of the worship space. It is the table around which we gather to offer the great prayer of thanksgiving and from which we receive the body and blood of the Lord. Historically it has always been known as the 'Lord's Table', the 'Holy Table', and has been associated with the traditions of the meal and the sacrifice of Christ. The earliest altars were simply tables of wood on which the gifts were placed during the liturgy; later tradition associated the altar with Christ's death and the tombs of the martyrs (which is why we retain the custom of enclosing their relics in or under it) and they became made of stone.

Today the altar should have a table-like quality which accentuates the symbolism of approachability to the Lord's Table and the sacrament of the eucharist. Normally it will be constructed of stone, which links it to the tradition of sacrifice and gives it a feeling of permanence. Because the theology of the liturgy stresses the symbol of the altar as a gathering point for the assembly with Christ at the eucharistic sacrifice, nothing that would detract from its primary function should be allowed to obscure the design. It should be free-standing, in its own spatial position; smaller, perhaps squarer in shape than in recent centuries, so that it does not dominate by sheer physical size; constructed to allow one person to celebrate at it with ease; and with enough room for the Missal and vessels for the eucharist to be placed on it. It should not be a repository for flowers or anything else apart from the things necessary for the celebration.

(e) The chair

The *chair* for the presider is meant to draw attention to the presidential role. This would seem to indicate that in many situations it should be positioned in the apex of the sanctuary space, historically its traditional position. However, this is dependent on the plan of the church, and in reordered churches there may be problems arising from existing features such as a preserved high altar or other architectural considerations. Whatever problem may occur, any confusion between the main focal points reduces the impact of the symbols themselves. Crowding the various foci means loss of clarity. The focus of the chair is intrinsic to the liturgical action; from the chair the introductory and concluding rites of the eucharist are performed and the homily may be preached from it. Because of the function of the presider as a symbol of Christ, the chair is a link between the two tables of the Word and sacrament and the assembly itself. It therefore needs its own spatial relationship to these areas. The presider must be given prominence and be visible to all those gathered. The chair should be a permanent sign linked through design to the other major foci but any attempt to create a throne-like structure must be firmly resisted.

(f) The reserved sacrament

Linked to the eucharistic action is the presence of the Lord in the eucharistic species. However, we need to remember that the purpose of reservation is primarily the distribution of communion to those who are sick, and secondly private devotion. These are both linked to the theology of the eucharist. It is not appropriate that this sign of Christ's presence be juxtaposed with the focal points of liturgical action, not because of any diminution of piety but because the major space of the church is designed for action, that is, the celebration of the eucharist. Because the Blessed Sacrament is a focus for (static) devotion, it should placed in its own space. Reserving it in a place apart is not relegating the sacrament to a secondary place; rather, it draws attention to the needs of the community for such a space in which to pray. Historically, reservation was a late development in the church building and the container for the sacrament took several forms – wall cupboard (aumbry), hanging pyx, sacrament house and tabernacle, to name a few. Today the directives concerning reservation suggest that the container should be solid, unbreakable and fixed. It should not be placed on an altar, for in keeping with liturgical theology and tradition there is only one altar in a church and that is a place for action, *not* reservation. As is customary, a lamp should burn continuously near it.

These liturgical symbols link the assembly together. The major foci of altar, ambo and chair are next in importance to the gathered community and for this reason the Church demands that great care be taken over their design and situation. The tendency to duplicate signs and objects and to lay a stress on secondary elements is detrimental to the function of these symbols themselves; that is why a full understanding of the nature of these focal points is important not only for the planning of a liturgical space, but for the understanding of the theology of the liturgical assembly itself.

Suitability for different liturgies

The main act of worship that lays claim to our attention and is therefore a determining factor in the design and art of our churches is the Sunday eucharist. Provision must always be made for the 'eucharistic room', a space suitable for the weekly celebration of the community. The General Instruction on the Roman Missal and the various instructions on liturgical space and its furnishings and art stress the importance of this celebration.

This does not mean that a building should be restricted to one activity or one particular style of celebration. Different forms of worship require alternative planning arrangements: for instance, smaller assemblies such as the weekday eucharist, and the larger festival and sacramental celebrations. All of these should enable those celebrating to participate in the liturgy without loss of a sense of gathering. In planning for these events the primary foci of the liturgy must retain their symbolic function as places of encounter.

The importance of movement within the assembly space and a certain flexibility of approach should enable various adjustments to be made. Marriage, for instance, is a family event; the action of the liturgy should take place in such a way that bride and groom are supported and physically surrounded by those who have come to witness and share in the celebration. The rites of initiation open out new possibilities for liturgical design, especially at the liturgy of baptism itself, where the action of pouring and immersion must be visible to those gathered. Not all churches will be able to offer possibilities of different arrangements for every type of occasion, but an understanding of the nature of the various forms of worship should help congregations, clergy and those involved in the planning and design of our buildings to create different environments within the one space. Here the careful use of various symbols and signs such as icons, banners and candles can create an ambience which will open out new possibilities. It is important too that the non-eucharistic liturgies are catered for, celebration of the Hours, reconciliation services, vigils and such like, so that the environment is used to increase the faith and life of the community.

CELEBRATION: THE LITURGY HANDBOOK

However, the building is not just a place for eucharistic and other forms of worship. The needs of specific groups must be considered. If it is the house of God's people, then the handicapped, elderly and children need to be catered for. The church is a house belonging to a place, a people and a time. The generosity of individuals and groups over the years will have given the building many of its furnishings and artefacts; some of these may have outlived their usefulness, others may inspire love and devotion. Therefore the devotional and pastoral life of the community will influence the way in which we perceive our space. This is why the provision of a sacrament chapel or distinct prayer area is invaluable. Then there are particular cults of saints, the stations of the cross and such like which need integration into the building, without intruding into the main eucharistic space or obscuring the main elements of that place. There will need to be a reconciliation room, an ambience demanding privacy and sensitive planning. Lastly, the ministry of hospitality demands that a place for gathering before and after the liturgy, so that people may be welcomed, exchange greetings and pass on information, is incorporated into the design. The symbolism of transitional movement, from the busy environment of everyday life into the atmosphere of celebration, communion and mystery, will help the vitality of our community life; entrances and exits are not simply practical, they have a function in speaking to us of our mission and our faith within the context of our world.

Design and brief

The environment of the liturgy gives the architect, pastor and community a brief which details the requirements for worship. Apart from this, it is the needs of the community as whole that must be taken into account, not only the perceived needs now but those for the future. A monolithic approach that designs a church for one purpose only will soon outlive its purpose; therefore simplicity of design, respect for the determinants and symbols of the liturgy and an awareness of the practical needs of the people would be the best approach. It is important that everybody is aware of the theology of the liturgy, the nature of the assembly and the importance of our primary and authentic symbols, as well as the importance of building a place for praying, singing, speaking and listening, where the mystery of God will be remembered and celebrated year by year. Our Church and its buildings cannot be cut off from life, we are called to serve the world and to act as pointers along the way of salvation. Therefore in the design and brief all the broader needs of the community, especially those of its suffering, disadvantged and handicapped members, must be taken into serious consideration.

In building or reordering a church, preparation and teamwork are essential components. Planning must be carried out according to the rules and regulations of the proper authorities, not for the sake of restriction, but because of the fundamental importance of the assembly and its liturgical action. The local church art and architecture committee should be available for guidance and help, so that competent people may assist in the consultation process. The clergy and congregation themselves must take time to be informed about liturgical theology and their own various needs and aware of their own competence, so that they will feel able to hand over the various areas of work to people who have shown understanding and care in the field of church art and architecture. In considering practicalities, special mention must be made of storage space, vestries, ancillary rooms and the various needs of those who require particular help, especially the deaf and disabled.

One of the primary requirements of worship is visibility. Any arrangement must take into account the proximity of what is seen so that nobody is too remote from the liturgical action. A second requirement is audibility. The demands of speech and song must be acoustically balanced and a well thought out audio system designed. Musicians and cantors need to be placed in a position where distortion is kept to a minimum, while the importance of proclaiming the Word requires that serious provision be made for microphones at the ambo, chair, altar, font and a few places in front of the congregation.

Human beings need a sense of scale to engender a feeling of belonging, hospitality and mystery. The architect, artists and designers must work with the congregation to achieve the best possible arrangements for facilitating common prayer and public worship. Unity of space does not mean uniformity in planning arrangements. The importance of vista, approach ways, light, darkness and different areas utilized within the space means that creativity can be exercised in constructing a sense of celebration, awe and mystery.

The exterior

The exterior image of our churches has traditionally been strong, with towers, steeples, large crosses and commanding buildings dominating the skyline. What was communicated was the importance and position of the church in that community. Today we need to be conscious of the message we are proclaiming in the unspoken symbols of our building. The image of triumphalism, ostentation and wealth is inappropriate for today. Sensitivity to the neighbourhood, and the mission of the Church, require a different approach. Often the cost of large buildings is prohibitive and many of our sites co-exist in a locality dominated by large-scale office blocks or domestic dwellings. Each design will need to take into account its position, the history and tradition of the locality and the way the Church envisages its role in that society. Therefore the external landscape will demand careful planning. The entrance way is important; is it welcoming, hospitable? Does it show a sense of community or project an image of isolation? Notice boards are an often overlooked part of the design. They are a means of communication, and their design and message will be of importance for those who see them. There is no reason to suggest that simplicity of design means bare necessity in any of our external details. Quality and appropriateness should be the hallmark of both our external and internal environments. Cheap, shoddy, fake or pretentious materials need to be avoided at all costs.

The total environment should be beautiful and engage the senses in sound, smell and vision so that people feel invited to enter and engage in the activity carried out there. One need only reflect on the symbol of the church bells in continental countries, how the sound awakens some resonance within us. This is the way symbols work. The cost of building need not be prohibitive; there are several examples of excellent churches built on a low budget, using local materials and local craftspeople, and it should always be borne in mind that good planning leaves room for future development.

Reordering

Our church buildings reflect a variety of styles; some are modern, some were constructed in previous ages. Because the liturgy and life of a people are never static, the requirements of contemporary situations will have to be met. The Church is not a curator of museum pieces but the custodian of history, living and growing today. The process of reordering poses theological as well as practical questions. It is important to examine the requirements of the liturgical assembly and then to see the artistic and historical merits of the building being considered. The present climate of architectural and artistic conservation favours great care and awareness of our heritage, but it is incumbent on all those concerned to make sure that the building is able to serve the assembly and its liturgy, not to constrain it with historicism. To help in these matters, various organizations at diocesan and national level have been, or are in the process of being, formed. The building as a whole can benefit by judicious and sensitive reordering or be destroyed by insensitivity. In some cases the rearrangement of the sanctuary space may be the only reordering necessary, but here again it is not just a question of provision for an altar facing the people, but a reappraisal of the central symbol of the altar and other major foci.

Care must always be taken of the determinants of the building and the patrimony of architecture and art. Some churches can benefit from a more visionary reordering; several of little or no particular merit could be axially reordered to great advantage. Each case must be taken on its own merits, but the procedures involved must take into account the dignity and beauty of the building and the nature and needs of the liturgy. There will be constraints: some places may have to contend with specific planning injunctions and requirements, especially if grants are obtained for restoration and maintenance work. That is why proper channels for proceeding with these matters have been set up, so that both the treasures of the past and the vision of the future may be safeguarded.

Furnishing

The different spaces in the church, sanctuary area and people's space require positive assessment. Any kind of monumentality or separation in terms of graded zones of holiness is to be avoided. However, the fixity of certain points needs to be evaluated. Normally the primary focal points of altar, ambo, chair and font will be fixed. In this way the eucharistic space is seen to be what it expresses. In designing, repairing or restoring any artefact or furnishing for the church one should bear in mind the practical needs of movement for different occasions. This also applies to the people's space. The liturgy is not a static event; posture and gesture play a large part in our prayer and worship. Not only must there be provision for seating in comfort, but access routes, processional paths, space to move about in, zones of space around the various foci all need to be carefully planned. The building should avoid clutter and congestion, a sense of gathering is achieved through a gradual process of assimilation, not through bunching together *en masse*. In all the furnishings for the liturgy there should be dignity and beauty in the design and form, colour and texture of the materials used. All the furnishings together should possess a harmony with each other and the architecture of the place. The Church demands that the symbols and furnishings used in worship should be of good quality, have a 'noble' simplicity and speak through their authenticity. If we exercise an evaluative and critical faculty, examining the basic requirements and the significance of what we are, then our symbols will speak: for example, the altar must be seen as a table and yet different from ordinary tables; the vesture of the president needs to be seen in terms of clothing, speaking through its form and texture rather than exterior decoration; the cross in place near the altar reflects our belief in Christ and his triumph over death; the candles we use

115

must be living flames; all our symbols and furnishings must be authentic and linked to our human lives. It is quality not quantity we need.

Liturgical art

Much more needs to be done in the field of liturgical art than we are doing at present. Too often we are hidebound by subjective influences that lead to the production of inferior and second-rate material. The function of art in the church is to enhance and uplift, to create a sense of beauty and order so that our senses may engage in that deeper encounter within. The Church has never made any particular style its own, but has constantly used what is best in the human experience. Therefore we should promote schemes to encourage better art in our church buildings and take care of what is beautiful and good from previous ages. All our art should be subject to the same evaluative criteria of quality and appropriateness. Certain embellishments which have become hindrances may need removing from our churches, to bring about a simplified and more austere interior space.

This brings into focus another area of creativity, the use of temporary decoration for particular celebrations, feasts and seasons. Banners and hangings are appropriate, so long as they do not degenerate into mere signboards. Their purpose, like that of all liturgical art, is to create an atmosphere and a mood by appealing to the senses, but they should never crowd the major focal points or obscure the ritual movement and action.

Within the liturgical space, decoration must not be confined to the sanctuary area alone, since the unity of the celebration space and the active participation of the assembly are fundamental principles. Beauty and simplicity demand a removal of things that have no use or are no longer in use. There must be no clutter or crowding; each object must function by itself. This will also involve a proper understanding and use of symbols. Too often, injudicious use is made of signs which are no longer appropriate or are confusing to contemporary society. Iconographic programmes and workshops must be encouraged, so that the skills of artists and craftspeople may be utilized in the service of the Church and the people of God. Within the local setting, the talents of those who can create should be put at the service of the community and the liturgical environment: drama and movement, textile decoration, floral designs, stained glass designs, all these play a part in creating an atmosphere of beauty and holiness. But in all cases the suitability, position and quality of anything connected with worship must be decided upon with proper and informed consultation. If, instead of serving the action of the assembly, it threatens, competes or confuses, then it must be removed. 'If an art form is used in liturgy it

116

must aid and serve the action of liturgy, since liturgy has is own structure, rhythm and pace' (*Environment and Art in Catholic Worship*). A major and continuing effort is needed among the believing community to restore respect for competence and expertise in all the arts; to be sensitive to the important place they have in enhancing our lives and bringing about an awareness of the sacred; and to win back to the service of the Church 'professional' people who too often have been replaced by commercial, mass-producing firms or volunteers whose work is inappropriate. The liturgy has special significance as a means of our relating to God, or of our response to God's love for us. Our response must be one of depth, authenticity, genuineness and care with respect for everything we use and do in the liturgical celebration.

DOCUMENTATION AND BIBLIOGRAPHY

Bishops' Conference of England and Wales, *The Parish Church* (London: CTS, 1984).

Constitution on the Liturgy, 122–129.

Environment and Art in Catholic Worship (Washington, DC: United States Catholic Conference, 1986).

General Instruction on the Roman Missal, 253–312.

Irish Episcopal Conference, *The Place of Worship: Pastoral Directory on the Building and Reordering of Churches* (Dublin: Veritas, 1991).

Publications by the Council for the Care of Churches, 83 London Wall, London EC2M 5NA.

Mark G. Boyer, *The Liturgical Environment: What the Documents Say* (Collegeville, MN: The Liturgical Press, 1990).

John Dillenberger, *A Theology of Artistic Sensibilities* (London: SCM Press, 1986).

Stephen and Cuthbert Johnson osb, *Planning for Liturgy: Liturgical and Practical Guidelines for the Reordering of Churches* (Farnborough: St Michael's Abbey, 1983).

A. G. Martimort, *The Church at Prayer*, vol. I: *Principles of the Liturgy* (London: Geoffrey Chapman, 1986).

Marchita Mauck, *Shaping a House for the Church* (Chicago: Liturgy Training Publications, 1990).

Unit 7

STEPHEN DEAN

LITURGICAL MUSIC

I. Theology of celebration

Singing is one of the most characteristic things done by Christians, or indeed by any religious people. This has been so from the beginning. The one place where the gospels talk of Jesus and his disciples singing is after the Last Supper: 'After the psalms had been sung, they left for the Mount of Olives' (Mark 14:26). At the very first eucharist, therefore, there was singing. And every day, all over the world, Christians are singing the praises of God. Joseph Gelineau sums it up thus: 'The Christian liturgy was born singing, and has never ceased to sing.' Pope Paul VI put it in more theological terms:

> The hymn of praise that is sung through all the ages in the
> heavenly places and was brought by the High Priest, Christ
> Jesus, into this land of exile has been continued by the Church
> with constant fidelity over many centuries, in a rich variety of
> forms.

Although gospel references to singing are minimal, song pervades the Bible. The characteristic biblical treatment of singing is an imperative: '*Sing* a new song to the Lord!' or, in St Paul, 'Sing each other songs, psalms and spiritual canticles' (Colossians 3:16; cf. Ephesians 5:19). Singing hymns was evidently part of the worship of the Corinthians (1 Corinthians 14:26), and Paul and Silas spent a night in prison praying and singing hymns (Acts 16:25). One whole book of the Bible is a collection of songs, and there are many other psalms, hymns and canticles embedded in both the Old and New Testaments. The book of Revelation shows the song of heaven.

We have early evidence of Christian song. The writer Pliny, sent by the Emperor Trajan to investigate the Christians, wrote back (*c.* AD 112) that they assembled on Sunday and 'sang a hymn to Christ as a God'. For the first centuries, the actual music that was sung is unknown to us, and likely to remain so; apart from a Greek fragment of the third century, the oldest surviving written Christian music dates only from the ninth to tenth centuries, and even then cannot be reliably interpreted. There are, however, texts. Hymns were probably sung by Christians before psalms; at least, there is no reference to psalm-singing before the third century. Rhythmical prose hymns such as the *Phōs Hilaron* and *Gloria in Excelsis* survive, as well as the metrical type made popular by St Ambrose. Hymns were also used by heretical groups, giving rise to the periodic suspicion of the use of non-scriptural material in the liturgy.

At first the whole congregation sang. Responsorial psalmody became popular from the fourth century, so the people sang in dialogue with a cantor, the oldest musical 'ministry'. The first choirs we hear about were choirs of girls or boys (later girls and women were barred from official ministry in music). As music grew in complexity it led to the replacement of congregational singing by that of trained singers. Although the Sanctus was still being sung by the people in some places up to the twelfth century, by the Middle Ages the choir had supplanted the people at Mass. Congregational singing survived in 'popular devotions', a situation found almost everywhere until the middle of this century, although Germany had a long tradition of vernacular hymns at Mass.

Pope Pius X in 1903 urged that singing at Mass should be restored to the people, but it took the Second Vatican Council to insist on it. The task of creating a tradition of singing at Mass has not been easy.

For most of history, and in most religions today, the place of singing has not been questioned. It is accepted as a normal part of human life and behaviour and, in the writings of the few theologians who have taken note of it, recognized and esteemed as a gift of God. It is only in recent times, and perhaps only since Vatican II in the Catholic Church, that we have had to think of reasons why we sing. Many Catholics have become used to a Mass without singing; although the distinction between 'Low Mass' and 'High Mass' is now obsolete and the GIRM only speaks of one sort of celebration, the spirit of 'Low Mass' is not dead. Some people speak of music as a distraction from prayer, a very different conception of the liturgy from those who consider that singing is itself prayer: 'the one who sings well, prays twice' (GIRM). There are also cultural problems with singing; in England people rarely sing together in public; many have been told from a young age that they 'can't sing'; and music has become something provided by professionals and listened to, rather than taken part in. In the Catholic Church (although not, as we shall see, at official level) there is a degree of suspicion about music and musicians. St Augustine, in a famous passage from the *Confessions*, agonized about the possible dangers of the sensuous element of music, and whether you should dare to *enjoy* it:

> Fierce I am sometimes, in the desire of having the melody of all pleasant music, to which David's psalter is so often sung, banished both from mine own ears, and out of the whole Church too: and the safer way it seems unto me ... Notwithstanding, as often as I call to mind the tears I shed at the hearing of thy church songs, in the beginning of my recovered faith, as long as I am moved not with the singing, but with the thing sung ... I then acknowledge the great good of this institution. Thus I float between the peril of pleasure, and approved profitable custom: inclined the more ... to allow of the old use of singing in the Church; that so by the delight taken in at the ears, the weaker minds be roused up into some feeling of devotion. (*Confessions* 10. xxxiii)

Nevertheless, the documents of the liturgical reform give singing an honoured place. GIRM says 'great importance should be attached to the use of singing at Mass', and justifies it by saying 'song is the sign of the heart's joy' (19). The heart represents the seat of our deepest feelings; if music can express these, it is powerful indeed. GIRM also quotes St Augustine: 'To sing belongs to lovers.' This may seem old-fashioned to us; although most operas and pop-songs are about love, our culture discourages us from breaking into song at the sight of our beloved. But almost everyone sings spontaneously on occasions, at times of particular emotion. Singing indicates lightness (or heaviness) of heart. It also helps a crowd to vent its euphoria, at a birthday party, at a football match – anywhere that people want to show strong feelings.

Feelings are often impossible to express in words. Music is its own language, not translatable into any other, and it can touch otherwise inaccessible regions of the soul. In times of grief music can give shape to the chaotic feelings of the bereaved. Art can portray the most tragic events in the most exquisite terms – witness the enduring popularity of the Requiem Mass and in particular the *Dies Irae*.

Singing, in short, is a human activity. A nineteenth-century Quaker hymn says 'How can I keep from singing?' and this sense of being impelled to sing makes it a natural part of worship. God has made us singing beings. To paraphrase St Augustine, 'to sing belongs to people', and it is something that people *should* do when addressing God; God evidently intends this delightful thing to be used. It is not a question of compulsion but of fullness of human response. Music is a gift of God; its use is both duty and delight. To sing is to let oneself go in more than a half-hearted fashion, and the strength of the singing is both an indication of the emotional temperature of a gathering and a means of its growth in faith and unity. The US Bishops, in their 1972 document *Music in Catholic Worship*, even said 'Faith grows when it is well expressed in celebration. Good celebrations foster and nourish faith. Poor celebrations may weaken and destroy it.'

Assembly

Music is something we do *together*. This has theological importance: to sing together people need to be present to and conscious of each other and strive to raise a single song to God. But togetherness works on a physical level as well. Shared melody and rhythm create a feeling of well-being. Rhythm, though certain kinds of it are regarded as suspect, even diabolical, is a vital part of music. The body itself has rhythms – the heartbeat, the breath – and musical rhythm can increase these or slow them down. Rhythm is also a help to memory.

Each song in a liturgy is part of the larger rhythm of ritual, the repetitive framework essential to maintaining continuity of worship. The liturgy is marked out by familiar sections, the Word and eucharist; the year by the reappearance of pieces like the *Exsultet* or 'Come, Holy Ghost', which hopefully will be greeted with pleasure and produce a positive response. The repetition of the rite given to us by the Lord, which we do in memory of him, is reinforced and made more powerful when music plays a central part in it.

Music in worship is always an action of the whole assembly. Because singing is, as said above, a means of *expression* (a sign of the heart's joy), the whole assembly should actually take some part in the singing; it has a right (and duty) to do so. The liturgy, though, is not a monologue but a conversation, and this is symbolized by 'conversational' ways of singing. There are dialogues between the presider and the assembly, such as the Preface dialogue. There are dialogues between the cantor or choir and the assembly, which may be part of the structure of a rite such as a penitential rite or responsorial psalm, or a device to aid participation such as a responsorial eucharistic acclamation. There is also choral singing or instrumental music for people to listen to. All music should aim towards the building up of the body of Christ in the service of the Word; it must be a means of promoting and expressing unity, not creating division. This unity is 'a unity of hearts through a unity of voices', as GIRM (56i) says of the communion song.

Mood

Since ancient times, one of music's most prized and mysterious attributes has been its capacity to affect people's state of mind, well-being or mood. The philosopher Boethius said: 'Nothing is more characteristic of human nature than its capacity for being soothed by sweet music and braced by strong music.' Plato and other writers prescribed particular 'modes' as socially acceptable and forbade others as producing unsuitable effects. Nowadays we may find this comic, but the power of music to control mood is exploited as much as ever. Every performer aims to produce certain emotional effects in the audience. Evidently, if good effects can be produced, so can malign ones. Music can quieten people or it can rouse them.

Liturgical musicians must resist trying to manipulate people, but should sing or play so that it is the liturgical action which draws the attention, not the performer. When purified of sinister and manipulative aspects, though, the mood-inducing function of music is an important one in the elements that go to make up liturgy, allowing people to express joy, lamentation or any other emotion.

It is a part of the skill of the leader of music, when planning a celebration, to take account of the effects the music might produce. Each piece should be seen as part of an ordered whole, preserving a balance between song, speech, silence, action and repose. Of course, planning can never produce precisely predictable results. Every celebration is the meeting of a people called together by God. God is not to be tied down by our calculations; he can breathe life into listless hearts and will expose mere show. Musicians should bear in mind the words of the prophet Amos (Amos 5:23).

Music is never an end in itself. Its success is ultimately measured not by how well we do it, but by whether it allows a genuine encounter with God.

II. Theology of music in liturgy

Music and Word

Music in Christian liturgy has, as Vatican II put it, a *munus ministeriale*, a role of ministry or service. It serves the people of God as a means of expressing their worship and of proclaiming the Word.

Many people resist the idea that music could be a servant, considering that art should be autonomous and free, but for a Christian believer everything is to be judged in the light of the Kingdom. Christian music must sing *about* Christ. In the beginning was the Word, and the Word was with God, and the Word was God. What we sing is an echo of that Word. The Liturgy Constitution emphasizes this as the basic function of liturgical music when it says that 'as sacred song *closely bound to the text*, [music] forms a necessary and integral part of the solemn liturgy' (112; author's italics). This is why singing is more important than instrumental music in Christian worship, and why at various times the authorities have made efforts to get people to sing the actual words of the liturgy, and preferably the actual words of Scripture, rather than free compositions.

What is it, specifically, that *Christian* song has to express? What is said about music by the Order of Christian Funerals (1990) could be taken as applying to any celebration:

> The texts of the songs chosen for a particular occasion should express the paschal mystery of the Lord's suffering, death, and triumph over death and should be related to the readings from scripture. (30)

There are many ways in which songs fail to live up to this requirement. The characteristic Christian pitfall is sentimentality; many hymns (not just in the Victorian era) give a picture of Christ that is unworthy of that given in the gospels. The Word addressed to us in Scripture is a two-edged sword which can lay bare the secrets of our hearts; it should not be wrapped in a bland and reassuring package which emasculates it. The best texts are scriptural in spirit, if not in actual words, and are matched to music that allows them to speak with appropriate force.

Music and rite

The Liturgy Constitution says music is integral to the liturgy. This is a strong word, almost (but not quite) implying that without music, the rite will not work. Of course, the rite will work without music; but not to sing at all, when singing is possible, is to mutilate the liturgy.

Music gives shape to words; it also gives shape to actions. Every liturgy is an action made up of a series of moments, such as proclamation, response, meditation, petition. The music of one part, for instance a penitential rite, can hardly be made to fit a contrasting one such as a eucharistic acclamation. At times in history the shape becomes distorted, for example by lengthy Glorias and Credos, two non-essential parts of the liturgy, and the original shape needs to be rediscovered.

But though it is easy to point to distortions, how do we decide what music is *good* for liturgy? The US Bishops in their document set out three questions to ask about any piece of music intended for use in celebration. In essence, they are: Is it any good as music? What is it for? Can people sing it? In other words, the musical judgement, the liturgical judgement and the pastoral judgement.

Musical judgement

Is the music any good? This is the ground on which most battles are fought. Everybody of course wants good music; no one strives for the bad. But aesthetic judgements are frequent causes of dispute. However, there are three important points to make in the case of liturgical music.

First, the questions of style and value are distinct. Liturgical music has used many styles and nowadays is using a wider range than before. This is quite legitimate. There is no such thing as a 'sacred' style, only styles which have become more associated with liturgy than others. Within each style there is good and bad music; the test of a piece is whether it gives adequate expression to the Paschal Mystery of Christ (see above). This point is not always grasped. Styles are judged *a priori*, resulting in the tragic and puzzling phenomenon of the body of Christ in a parish being split into different congregations who never meet and who define themselves in terms of the music they favour rather than of the one Lord they serve.

Second, though all liturgical music should strive to be good, not all good music is liturgical. Since the Renaissance the arts and the Church have followed parallel paths, and what is good is not the same as what is suitable. A Haydn string quartet is always good, but not liturgical. The promotion of active participation has meant that much of the former repertoire is no longer compatible with the needs of the liturgy – a cause of distress to some. To determine what is liturgical, some terminology may help; music used in the liturgy is most accurately described as *ritual music*, which distinguishes it from 'sacred music', 'religious music' or even 'church music'.

Third (despite the foregoing), SC mentions the duty of preserving the heritage of sacred music (114). It should be assumed that, in stating this requirement, the bishops were filled with the pastoral concern which inspired the whole of the Council. Preservation *for its own sake* is not a primary purpose of the liturgy. However, one should esteem the beautiful as a reflection of God and not despise it. Moreover, by continuing to use music from past centuries, where it is appropriate, we keep in touch with those who have gone before us; it is not healthy to sing *only* music written in the last ten years. This is not to confuse liturgy and education. Liturgy's prime object is that God should be praised in spirit and truth by a people who understand what they are doing; other ways can be found of preserving the heritage, such as concerts.

Liturgical judgement

This deals with the question of function. Each part of the liturgy has its function in the whole, and these functions vary. Some sung parts accompany an action, such as processional songs or the 'Lamb of God' (which accompanies the breaking of bread). Some are rites in themselves, such as the Gloria, or the responsorial psalm. In each rite some purpose is to be accomplished: God is praised, or thanked, or we lament our sinfulness; and the music is to be judged by whether it enables these actions to take place or hampers them.

It is not simply that the action is accomplished. The music should help it to be accomplished *better*. An acclamation can acclaim better if sung. In English culture, which is more concerned with listening to music than taking part in it, music is thought of as an optional extra, something to fill in gaps; hence the 'hymn-sandwich' Mass which emphasizes peripheral elements at the expense of the central. Those whose experience of music at Mass is limited to this never get the chance to discover what music really can accomplish.

It would be convenient to demonstrate this by saying 'You can't *say* Alleluia', but many people do just that. A better example is the work of Taizé, in which text and music form an inseparable unit. There is no question of not singing – to *recite* the response would be absurd. But unless the singing becomes a prayer, people tire of the music. It can only work as an integrated ritual of sung prayer, in which the singing is a means of lifting the heart to contemplation and the music is no longer perceived as the foreground element but as the vehicle. Something similar can sometimes be conveyed by a familiar, hackneyed hymn. At a funeral, 'The Lord's my Shepherd' acquires a meaning it rarely has otherwise.

LITURGICAL FORM. The function of a piece determines its *form*. After Vatican II the hymn-with-verses form was seized upon and squeezed out other possible approaches such as the psalm/refrain form. Countless more songs have followed, not just in the 'traditional' but also in the 'folk' style which by the late 1960s had taken root in England from its starting point in the USA. However, this kind of song is an interloper in the Mass. The strophic hymn is a 'closed' form. It works best as a doctrinal statement in lyrical form (the hymns of Charles Wesley are an outstanding example) not accompanying an action, but as a rite in itself which allows due attention to be given to the words.

In the Roman liturgy hymns are most at home in the Liturgy of the

Hours, where these conditions occur. In the Mass they tend to be more effective at times when people can attend to the words, such as the preparation of the gifts and after communion. To accompany an action, more 'open' forms, which can be varied in length, are preferable, such as a litany or a song with cantor's verses and congregational refrain. 'Lamb of God', the song accompanying the breaking of bread, is an example. This action may vary considerably in length and the cantor needs extra invocations to sing. This principle applies to other parts of the Mass.

Naturally, the text must also be appropriate. At a Mass without singing, the Missal texts are usually adhered to, but singing opens the door to all sorts of possibilities. This can result in responsorial psalms which are not psalms, 'offertory songs' which support an obsolete view of this rite, a thousand rewritings of the Sanctus to fit a favoured tune, and so on. A composer must always be faithful to the liturgy and Scripture.

The question of 'form' also includes the question of who sings – the priest, the cantor or choir in dialogue with the rest, or the whole assembly. This could be a question of convenience, or it could be symbolic. In the case of the introductory dialogue to the Preface, for example, the priest is summoning the community to prayer, so the dialogue form is essential.

STRUCTURE – FLOW – BALANCE. Music has a shaping function, not only within a particular rite, but in the liturgy as a whole. Singing is not the only means of proclaiming a text. A wholesale return to sung readings is unlikely, and the Eucharistic Prayer is more often recited than sung. The alternation of sung and spoken texts and, very importantly, silence is part of the pattern of the Mass which the presider and leaders of music should be adept at handling.

The Missal of Paul VI gives far greater freedom of choice than its predecessor, but also heaps more responsibility on those who plan and lead the celebration. The revision due to be completed by the mid-1990s goes even further. The introductory rites will require much thought. Is a 'rousing entrance hymn' possible for people coming in straight off the street after a week without meeting? Does too much happen at the beginning of Mass? This period of intense activity is followed by a lessening of tension, just when the first major section of the Mass, the Liturgy of the Word, begins. Similarly, after the Sanctus the singers relax, everyone kneels down and the Eucharistic Prayer may become simply a background noise. We need to learn to draw attention to the central parts and away from the peripheral. Overloaded entrance rites should not distract from the Liturgy of the Word. The preparation of the gifts does not *need* any singing; it should be a moment of relative repose before the Eucharistic Prayer which should be participated in actively. Communion is often mishandled musically: the function of the 'Lamb of God' as an accompaniment to the breaking of bread is often not grasped; the attempt to stimulate singing during the communion procession is seldom made; and the option of a thanksgiving hymn (GIRM 56j) instead of a recessional is overlooked.

PRIORITIES. Liturgical judgement also comes into play in planning a long-term programme of music. A parish may decide to introduce music at a Mass which has not hitherto had any singing. It is decided to start with the familiar, a well-known hymn or song, 'just to get people started'. As long as things don't remain at this level, a case can be argued for this. If a hymn-sandwich threatens to become permanent, warning bells should ring.

The Bishops' Music Committee chart *Music in the Mass* sets out in schematic form the priorities for singing, as implied or made explicit in documents such as GIRM. In the first (most essential) category are not hymns, but acclamations: the gospel acclamation and the acclamations of the Eucharistic Prayer. The four classic 'hymn slots' are only found on level 3. This is not to say they are third-rate; rather, it means that if you get stuck on level 3 and never make an attempt to introduce levels 1 and 2 you are distorting the liturgy.

To avoid this, planning is necessary, inspired not by an abstract idea of liturgy, but by a pastoral outlook of concern for the people of the parish.

There can be *too much* music. GIRM says 'It is not always necessary to sing all the texts that are of themselves meant to be sung' (19). However, it should always be the most significant parts that are given preference.

Pastoral judgement

The music must be within the capacity of the community to sing, or to benefit from listening to it. There should be some means of discovering what this is. Musicians frequently decide *a priori* what people can or cannot sing and become impatient with congregations, usually because they forget how 'non-musicians' see music. Comments need to be interpreted; people use non-musical terms which the musician finds difficult to grasp, or express sweeping 'likes' and 'dislikes'. Even these need interpretation; often a particular piece is disliked because of the way it was presented.

Music should be chosen not for simple considerations of likes or dislikes, however, but to enable the community to express its faith. People respond readily (a) if they can see a reason for doing something and (b) if it is evident that it is connected with *prayer*. The reason for choosing a hymn or song, particularly a new one, needs to be explained. New music should be taught directly to the people; this teaching should not disturb the prayerful atmosphere, and over-frequent introduction is not appreciated. (When something new is sung, judgement should be made afterwards as to whether it worked, and if not, why.)

However, though the pastoral judgement is a reminder to consider the whole assembly at all times, it should not be used to restrict people to a diet of the safe and familiar. The musicians can draw on a wider knowledge than most of the congregation, and should share it with them as an enrichment of their celebration and of the means they have to express their faith.

Music and community

The community dimension of music is implied by everything that has been said so far. If music is not a means of unity in the people of God, it is nothing. If it is a means of *disunity*, God forbid. We have too easily accepted the notion of parishes fragmented by varied musical tastes, the 'market-place' phenomenon. People can shop around for a Mass which suits them; the bare fact of going to Mass is valued, not the oneness of the people of God. In some places all the musicians come together for great feasts but often there is confrontation rather than tolerance and willingness to compromise. If liturgy planning is co-ordinated at parish level rather than being left to self-contained groups, and if the parish as a whole can contribute ideas, these virtues will have a chance of developing. The leaders must have a vision which allows them to see beyond narrow limits. For some people music has become *too* important; they cling to a particular style so fiercely that if deprived of it they may break off from the community altogether. This is most unsatisfactory. Everyone must feel valued, both in themselves and for the gifts they can offer to the parish. This leads to the question of ministry.

III. Theology of ministry

Ministry as relationship

Recent years have seen a ministry 'explosion'; any task done on behalf of the community is dignified by the name of ministry, with varying degrees of formality. In the case of musicians the word 'ministry' is used in an honorific sense, to give value to what musicians do and inculcate a spirit of service. The task of the musician lends itself to domination; the idea of service is not easy for musicians, who necessarily measure their results in terms of the effects they produce. A liturgical musician must be self-sacrificing and desire to produce effects in people which will be beneficial to *them*, i.e. helping to open their minds to the presence of God and enabling them to worship in spirit and truth.

Liturgical musicians have to deflect attention from themselves and towards God; they must be 'transparent'. Until shortly before his death in 1992, one could walk into the church of Ste Trinité in Paris on Sunday and hear a great composer, Olivier Messiaen, playing the organ at Mass. A casual visitor would not have known who it was. Liturgical musicians have to put their gift at the service of the community and not expect to be thanked for it, although this is a bonus.

Naturally, some musical tasks in the assembly involve leadership, notably those of the organist, cantor and leader of song. This must be seen as part of a framework of collaborative ministry. The musician has a unique task; but so does the reader, so does the eucharistic minister, and, of course, the priest. They are not to see each other as competing for the top spot but as being incomplete without each other. Their ministries only exist because of the needs of the community.

This last point – the needs of the community – works both ways. If there is no-one to supply these needs, the community should look for such people. The Catholic Church in Britain has taken few steps to provide a supply of musicians; it simply expects them to turn up. Only a few dioceses have a musical director or adviser. There is no official means of training, nor any recognized standard to achieve. The value of the volunteer tends to be perceived as greater than that of someone trained for the job.

Training needs to be done professionally, whether it consists of lessons from a local organist or guitarist, a summer school or residential weekend, or a degree course. Parishes should be prepared to sponsor musicians, particularly the young. Then, having acquired music leaders, the parish needs to reward them suitably. To plan and carry out the music for liturgy, even one Mass a week, can occupy a great amount of time.

Liturgical music ministries

THE ASSEMBLY. The primary singer of the song is the whole people of God. Early Christian writers used the metaphor of the stringed instrument, every string contributing a note to the general harmony, to describe the assembly. Every liturgical action is an action of the whole people of God with Christ as its head. The active participation which this demands from us, individually and collectively, cannot be delegated to anyone.

THE PRESIDER. The presider or priest is the primary animator of the celebration. In all rites there are parts assigned to the presider to sing, either dialogues with the assembly or texts for proclamation. The Eucharistic Prayer, which begins and ends with dialogue and contains long passages of proclamation, illustrates both kinds. Penitential Rite 3 is another dialogue and may also include a cantor's part. The Missal also includes tones for the presidential prayers, the readings and the various dialogues during the Mass. Other ritual occasions have sung parts; there are several in Holy Week and the Triduum, such as the blessing of water at the Easter Vigil.

Priests should be encouraged to sing their part, as this adds to the festive character of the celebration and encourages everyone else. It is not necessary to sing everything (see GIRM 19), so an order of priorities should be established, with the Preface dialogue and the doxology of the Eucharistic Prayer at or near the top and the presidential prayers low down. Recent documents on seminary training have emphasized the need for future priests to receive instruction in music.

Besides singing their own parts, priests can stimulate the singing by being seen to join in the parts everybody sings. To do otherwise suggests that singing is something to keep the people busy while the real action is going on elsewhere.

THE DEACON. Similar considerations apply to the deacon, who can proclaim the gospel dialogue, the gospel and the dismissal. Like the presider, the deacon should be seen to join in the parts everybody sings.

THE CANTOR. The office of cantor is very ancient. It has several apsects: there is the *leader of song* aspect (GIRM says (64) 'there should be a cantor or a choirmaster to direct and encourage the people in singing'). There is the *teaching* aspect: new music should be introduced and explained to the congregation. This involves the very important skill of teaching music to people without technical musical knowledge; if this skill is lacking, the teaching may fail to achieve its result. This reinforces the notion that congregations can't or won't sing, which can often be disproved by putting on 'Soul of my Saviour'. Congregations *can* sing if given the right support.

Uniting both these aspects is the *leader of prayer* function. A possible ancestor of the cantor is a figure found in the synagogue in ancient times, the *sheliach tzibbur*, a volunteer prayer leader. The cantor is someone who prays, and helps the assembly to pray.

The cantor may also be the *psalmist*. The psalm is part of the Liturgy of the Word, and the offices of psalmist and reader are related. The psalmist should study the psalms to make their proclamation more effective.

THE CHOIR. The choir as we know it, a group of skilled people set apart and singing technically advanced music, is a late developer, only reaching its modern form in the late Middle Ages when the congregation had ceased to sing at Mass. Its subsequent history is bound up with that of Western musical art, of which it was in some senses the cradle. But the scene was set for a clash, and when the Council endorsed the notion of active participation, the function of the choir and the repertoire they had built up over centuries was put into question.

The choir has had certain limits put on its role; there are parts of the Mass (e.g. the Sanctus) which are directed to be sung by everybody (GIRM 55). The common justification of the choir that it leads the people is often disproved in practice; since it produces a more rehearsed sound, this often awes the rest into silence. However, a skilled choir is something to be prized. It introduces a dimension of artistic sound in the assembly which can be integrated into the celebration, greatly enriching it without diminishing everyone else's participation. The choir's contribution includes not only descants and choral harmonies to pieces which everyone sings, but also motets and anthems which extend and make more effective the proclamation of the Word. Choirs can also give concerts at which music whose use in the liturgy can no longer be justified is performed.

Choirs can be 'schools' of music in a parish (in Latin, *scholae*). They are a training ground for cantors and accompanists. They provide an opportunity for children to take an active part in the liturgy.

The correct position of the choir is important, not only for acoustic reasons but because it influences the choir's attitude to its ministry. It is hard for choristers to see themselves, and for others to see them, as part of the assembly if they are in a place far removed from everyone else (see GIRM 274).

It is recommended that choirs should pray together at practices and prepare spiritually at greater length for major celebrations.

These remarks apply not only to 'traditional choirs' but any sort of singing group including 'folk' groups; all special groups bring the same benefits and have to guard against the same pitfalls.

INSTRUMENTALISTS. The human voice is the primary instrument in the liturgy, because it can proclaim the Word. At first the Church was greatly suspicious of instruments but in the West they have been in use for many centuries. The organ has developed along with the liturgy and is the 'traditional' instrument in church (SC 120), but practically every kind of instrument has been used at some time. Though there were restrictions in the past, today there are none except common sense and musical and liturgical appropriateness.

Instrumentalists, like all musicians, must cultivate an attitude of service. Their most important job is to accompany the assembly, who cannot be treated in the same way as a rehearsed group of singers. Accompaniment is a particular skill not always possessed by solo performers. The assembly must be given adequate support – a single guitar is rarely sufficient – and neither hurried nor slowed down. Accompaniment is most effective when the people do not notice it. Organists in particular should resist the urge to dominate, by volume or the use of over-elaborate arrangements.

COMPOSERS. In spite of all the work put into the revised texts and rituals it has often proved difficult to translate the words on the page into effective means of celebration. Some parts of the new Mass, such as the penitential rite and the eucharistic acclamations, have been, effectively, new creations. It is not sufficient to tell people they must acclaim; it needs a composer to provide the vehicle by which this may be done; and in doing so, the limitations of the written text are often exposed. Composers have taken the development of the liturgy forward as a result of the experience of trying to clothe it with song, and this is likely to continue. It cannot be said that we have reached a totally satisfactory stage of development of, say, the responsorial psalm.

The role of the composer should be valued and appreciated. Most composers are active parish musicians, and could be given leisure to write if they were properly paid. Another way in which the church could support composers is to refrain from photocopying their music without permission and without payment, which apart from any other considerations is against the law.

Ministry as prayer

Liturgical musicians are not always encouraged to see what they do as prayer. Inevitably, they are preoccupied with getting the notes right and, when they have done so, with receiving approval. There is an understandable tendency to become self-centred and, indeed, a desire to excel is necessary to a performer. A spirituality which will help liturgical musicians live their vocation still needs to be developed. No-one has yet become a canonized saint through being a musician.

Cultivating an attitude of service is a lifelong task. The way to start is for musicians, first, to see themselves as part of the assembly and not a separate group; and, second, to listen to the Word of God and take it to heart, and take part inwardly and outwardly in the Eucharistic Prayer. It is not right to say you are *too busy to pray*, nor that the need to be alert and have the next piece ready prevents you from listening to what is going on. Musicians should practise everything in great detail before the celebration begins so that they are not constantly worrying about the music.

Choirs and groups of musicians should pray regularly and have days of recollection where they can discuss their ministry and listen to the guidance of Scripture. There is no biblical doctrine of music as such, but in fact the whole Bible is for musicians, for whom the greatest commandment is the same as for everybody else: 'Love God, and love your neighbour as yourself.'

The spirit of service works in both ways. The Christian community is made up of people who should learn to support each other. A parish must support its ministers and understand the pressures they are under. Misunderstandings and hostilities between clergy and musicians are regrettably common, for instance when a new priest arrives. If musicians are told they are no longer wanted their very faith can take a blow and they stop going to Mass.

Amen

The book of Revelation gives us a glimpse of the heavenly liturgy, where Hosanna is sung ceaselessly before the throne of God. We are privileged to raise a faint echo of this glorious praise by using the voices God has given us. It is our duty and our delight. Beyond the human aspects of music – its ability to bring us together, to make the words memorable and to add festivity – and beyond the ritual functions of music which allow the liturgy to be shaped, there is a symbolic purpose to music. It points to the beyond.

DOCUMENTATION AND BIBLIOGRAPHY

Constitution on the Liturgy, ch. 6.

General Instruction on the Roman Missal, esp. 19.

Music in the Mass, Bishops' Conference of England and Wales Church Committee leaflet (1987).

US Bishops' Committee on the Liturgy, *Liturgical Music Today* (Washington, DC: United States Catholic Conference, 1982).

Virgil C. Funk (ed.), *Music in Catholic Worship: The NPM Commentary* (Washington, DC: Pastoral Press, 1983).

Joseph Gelineau, *Learning to Celebrate: The Mass and Its Music* (Washington, DC: The Pastoral Press, 1985).

CELEBRATION: THE LITURGY HANDBOOK

Lawrence J. Johnson, *The Mystery of Faith: The Ministers of Music* (Washington, DC: The Pastoral Press, 1983).

Unit 8

PAULINE CLARKE

THE LITURGY OF THE HOURS

Introduction

The titles 'Liturgy of the Hours' or 'Prayer of the Church' are the preferred names for this prayer, replacing 'Divine Office' ('divine duty') and 'Breviary' ('briefer form'). The title 'Prayer of the Church' indicates that this form of prayer is for all: clergy, religious and laity. The title 'Liturgy of the Hours' suggests that certain times of the day express a quality common to all times and hours through which is revealed the mystery of Christ.

The Hours offer us, as well, a pattern of prayer to underpin our daily lives. Anyone wishing to study the Prayer of the Church would do well to begin by reading the General Instruction on the Liturgy of the Hours (GILH), which offers a clear pastoral, spiritual and theological introduction. Another very important initiation would be to celebrate the Liturgy of the Hours with others; to pray it, savour it and gradually identify with it. The celebration of Evening Prayer on Sundays and major feasts in the parishes is a splendid reminder that the Liturgy of the Hours is first and foremost a celebration.

The power of the Liturgy of the Hours

The Church expresses its prayer in different ways. One way is through the celebration of the eucharist and other sacraments; another is through the Prayer of the Church. With the help of the Holy Spirit, we enter into the Paschal Mystery of Christ and contemplate an aspect of this mystery according to the pattern of the liturgical year. The Liturgy of the Hours is prayer celebrated in common, based on Scripture, put together according to certain structural laws which facilitate group prayer while affording the individual an opportunity for some silent contemplation. Our horizons are constantly being extended as we celebrate the many different moments of the liturgical year. For example, on Christmas Day we are shown how the promises of the Old Testament are fulfilled in Christ; we see the effect of Christ's birth

135

on the Church as a whole and on each individual. This provides us with a counterpoint to the Lectionary at Mass.

The Prayer of the Church is a constant source of adoration, praise, thanksgiving and intercession. As we celebrate it, our life in God, received at baptism, gradually unfolds and develops. It is prayer which is God-directed, not self-centred, though intercession for the whole world has an integral part. Not only is it the prayer of the Christian community, indwelt by Christ and inspired by the Holy Spirit; it is in fact the prayer of Christ, in his Church, interceding for us with the Father. He is praying with us and for us, praying in us as our head while we pray to him as our God. He prays for us as our eternal High Priest (cf. SC 7, 83 and GILH 3). Thus we are in communion with him, with one another, with the Church throughout the world, and with the Church in heaven.

When we turn on the radio or television, the programme is already being broadcast and we tune in, becoming part of it. This is a useful parallel with the Hours, in which we tune into a liturgy that is ceaselessly expressed by Christ and the Church throughout the world. As we shall see, Morning and Evening Prayer are the hinges on which this continuous prayer turns, being most intimately linked with our natural rhythm of rising and resting, sunrise and sunset. A mother of eight children recently wrote:

> Morning and Evening Prayer of the Church I need as faithful companions of many years standing: they root me in the wider Church – past, present and future, and get me out of my narrow orbit. When I say the Prayer of the Church I feel I can safely throw myself, with all my pettiness, into this vibrant tide of praise and supplication.[1]

Historical development

It is widely assumed that there is direct continuity between Jewish prayer in the synagogue and the temple and primitive Christian prayer in common, but the evidence is not universally accepted. Several systems of daily prayer existed in Judaism at the time of the New Testament: the *Shema* ('Hear, O Israel ...': Deuteronomy 6:4–9 and elsewhere) was recited twice daily, morning and evening, with accompanying benedictions or prayers of thanksgiving. A quite different custom included benedictions three times a day: morning, afternoon and evening.

The New Testament describes how Jesus and his disciples, practising members of the Jewish community, attended the synagogue and participated in its liturgies. As Luke tells us, Jesus went to the synagogue in

Nazareth as was his custom (Luke 4), took an active part in the liturgy and was asked to preach. He also offered praise, adoration, thanks and petition to the Father, *abba*, at all the significant moments in his life (e.g. Matthew 11:25–26; Mark 14: 32–39; Luke 10:21–22; and John 17), and he commanded his disciples to pray (e.g. Matthew 5:44; Mark 13:33; Luke 6:28). After Jesus' ascension the disciples were continually in the temple praising God (Luke 24:53) and on his missionary journeys Paul regularly went to the synagogue when he arrived in a town (Acts 13, 14 and 17; etc.). Other texts suggest that from the beginning the Christians tended to form a distinct group within Judaism and to worship apart, e.g. in the upper room of a private house (Acts 1:13–14; 2:1; 4:23–31) and at night in the house of John Mark (Acts 12). Even in the temple, the Christians gathered in Solomon's portico, separating themselves from the rest. Although it would seem that constant and daily prayer was characteristic of the earlier Christians, it is difficult to claim that daily common prayer can be proved, with certainty, from the New Testament. It can be said that it was the rule in the synagogue, that the first Christians continued to attend the synagogue and that it is likely, therefore, to have been the custom in the Church.[2]

When we move beyond the earliest generations of Christians, the evidence regarding daily prayer in the communities is fragmentary until the fourth century. Early Christian writings, e.g. the *Didache* (*c.* 70), the *Apostolic Tradition* of Hippolytus (*c.* 215), Tertullian's *Treatise on Prayer* (160–225) and the writings of Cyprian of Carthage and Clement of Alexandria (150–215), testify to the importance of prayer, morning and evening. References were made by some of these writers to a ritualizing of the lighting of the evening lamps, possibly symbolizing Christ as the light of the world. Further, it was suggested that the rising sun symbolized the risen Christ who was expected to return. The Paschal Mystery of Christ, his Passover from death to life, was thus evoked in morning praise and evening thanksgiving. In some communities there was also prayer at the third, sixth and ninth hours and again during the night.

The Peace of Constantine in the fourth century, granting religious freedom to Christians, enabled the development of structured prayer in common in local churches throughout the Mediterranean. This public prayer became known as the Cathedral Office,[3] centred on the local bishop with at least a representative number of people. Morning and Evening Prayer were celebrated daily; Psalm 62(63) was used at Morning Prayer and Psalm 140(141) at Evening Prayer. Several sources provide evidence of additional elements, e.g. a lucernarium (service of light) to begin Evening Prayer.[4] Sources from the fourth to the eighth centuries speak of more psalms and biblical canticles morning and evening, including Psalm 50(51) and Psalms 148–150, the canticle of the three young men on Sundays and on feast days, and the Gloria during Morning Prayer. There would be intercessions, a blessing and a dismissal. Evening Prayer which included a lucernarium often contained the evening hymn *Phōs Hilaron*, 'O radiant light', evening psalms, incense, intercessions, blessings and a dismissal. There is evidence of a weekly night vigil Office celebrating the Lord's resurrection. The pattern and content of the Cathedral Office was almost entirely invariable, it related to the time of day when it was celebrated and included strong symbolism such as candles, incense, darkness and light; usually without readings, it was predominantly a prayer of praise, thanksgiving, adoration and petition.

The rise of monasticism and the influence of the Desert Fathers introduced profound changes in Christian spirituality and liturgical practice. Instead of set psalms appropriate to the time of day, the monks recited the whole of the psalter continuously. They devoted much time throughout the day and night to a heavy schedule of long periods of formal community prayer which became known as the Monastic Office. The most common pattern included the following Hours or times of prayer: the Night Office and seven day Offices: Matins, Lauds (Morning Prayer), Prime, Terce (9am), Sext (noon), None (3pm), Vespers (Evening Prayer) and Compline (Night Prayer). All these included many psalms recited responsorially and antiphonally, a reading from Scripture (from St Paul) and a gospel, probably a gospel canticle and also intercessions. It would be a mistake to assume that the prayer of the people – the Cathedral Office – and the prayer of the monks were in opposition: they were different and they were complementary. Many monastic communities adopted the cathedral Morning and Evening Prayer, celebrating them in different ways; sometimes adding psalms or simply taking them as they were. In the great pilgrimage centres such as Jerusalem, Rome, and Caesarea in Cappadocia, the two forms gradually merged and the faithful were encouraged to join in the longer hours of the monastic-type Office, celebrated in the basilicas.

In the course of time, the influence of the monks predominated; from among their ranks the local bishop was chosen, and the administration, organization and liturgical life of the parish was in their hands. As the monks established communities across Europe, the Divine Office, as celebrated in the monasteries, established itself and gradually replaced the office of the people. There was a tendency to lengthen it, overload the contents of the Hours and distance their celebration from the natural rhythms of the day and night. In St Columban's *Rule of Monks* one learns of an Irish monastic Office in which there are almost a hundred psalms. The tradition of reciting the complete psalter was firmly established. The Rule of St Benedict introduced some modifications in the length of the Hours and it is from this source that the pattern of the Divine Office became established and celebrated, with adjustments from time to time, until our own day.

The obligation for all clergy to celebrate the Hours in each church gradually became the norm during the eighth and ninth centuries. Between the eleventh and fifteenth centuries, offices might be celebrated twice on feast days. There were various additions: hymns at all the Hours, extensions to Prime, Offices of the Dead and Our Lady, lengthy prayers, more psalms and more suffrages for the dead. 'Pray at all times' (1 Thessalonians 5:17) was taken literally and the notion spread that the more one added to the Office, the holier one would become. All this made the performance of the Office a burden for the clergy and an impossibility for the laity. It was celebrated in a language they no longer understood; it was too complicated by far and too remote from the people. Gone were the days when everyone knew the Hours by heart and participated fully in their celebration.

Lay people began to focus on popular devotions such as the rosary and the Angelus. There were collections of parts of the Office in primers and in books of the Hours. Still later, manuals of piety became very popular among the laity. Relief for some clergy was found in shorter Offices which appeared from time to time, notably the thirteenth-century Office of the Roman Curia which was itself an abridged form (breviary) of the Roman Office used by the Pope and his household. Dispensations from choral celebrations multiplied and consequently the private recitation of the Hours, often bunched together with no reference to the time of day, soon became the norm.

Efforts to reform the Office followed in the fifteenth and sixteenth centuries, but these were frowned upon by the Council of Trent (1545–63) which restored a version of the Office of the old Roman basilicas. This was the Roman Breviary of 1568, which banned the use of all modified forms unless they were more than two hundred years old. All was directed, for the most part, to private recitation, even though choral celebration continued to exist in cathedrals, some parishes and monasteries. Despite minor reforms, the structure and content of the Roman monastic Office remained essentially the same until 1911, when Pope Pius X sought to abolish certain abuses and wished to re-establish a balance. The psalms were redistributed, sometimes divided, and the number for each day reduced. In November 1911 *Divino Afflatu* decreed what was intended to be the first stage of a complete reform of the Office. This was continued, in part, during the pontificates of Pius XI and Pius XII. The study of much-needed reform was thorough, but on the whole reforms were few. Under Pope John XXIII the Preparatory Liturgical Commission for the Second Vatican Council drew up a schema for the reform of the liturgy which included a chapter on the Office. Their work was approved and became the basis of chapter 4 of the Constitution on the Liturgy. The following extracts illustrate the points of departure for the revision of the Hours which followed the Council:

> The Divine Office, as it has come down from ancient Christian tradition, is so composed that the whole course of day and night is consecrated by praise offered to God. Since the end of the Office is the sanctifying of the day, the traditional cycle of the hours will be restored in such a way that, as far as possible, its true correspondence in time shall once more be given to each hour. (SC 84 and 88)

Lauds (Morning Prayer) and Vespers (Evening Prayer) were to be considered the chief hours; Compline to be made a fitting end to the day; Prime would be abolished and Matins revised to become the Office of Readings; Terce, Sext and None were to be maintained, but the option to recite one of these, corresponding closely to the time of day, was to be introduced (see Article 89). The post-conciliar Commission incorporated the directives of chapter 4 of the Constitution into its work of revision and went even further. The revised Liturgy of the Hours would be a better Office and would encourage the faithful to join in the communal celebration of the chief Hours – Morning and Evening Prayer (see GILH 20, 27). 'The Liturgy of the Hours is not a private matter but belongs to the whole body of the Church whose life it both expresses and affects' (GILH 20); 'Lay groups gathering for prayer, apostolic work, or any other reason are encouraged to fulfil the Church's duty by celebrating part of the Liturgy of the Hours' (GILH 27).

The Commission chose to retain the essentially monastic structures of the Office even though the possibility for radical revision was open to them. They achieved much after long and painstaking work. The psalms are now distributed over a four-week cycle and organized appropriately at the various hours; the Office of Readings may take place at any time, and its readings are fully revised; a hymn now begins each Hour; the number of biblical canticles, both Old and New Testament, has increased and the invitatory psalm is transferred from the Office of Readings to Morning Prayer (if this is the first Hour of the day). The structure of all the Hours has been simplified and made more uniform in order to bring the Liturgy of the Hours back within everyone's reach.

The content and structure of Morning and Evening Prayer especially will be considered in detail. Before proceeding to these aspects, we shall examine the theology of the Liturgy of the Hours.

Theology

Christian worship is not how we seek to contact God: it is a celebration of how God has touched us, has united us to himself and is ever-present to us and dwelling in us. It is not a reaching-out for a distant reality but a joyful celebration of a salvation that is just as real and active in the ritual celebration as it was in the historical event. It is ritual in which the symbolic action is not a memorial of the past but a participation in the eternally present Paschal Mystery. In a nutshell, liturgical spirituality is simply accepting God. This is expressed in chapter 1 of *Sacrosanctum Concilium*, notably in articles 5 and 6.[5]

This then is the meaning of all our liturgies: Christ's victory and triumph over death for which we give unending thanks to the Father through the power of the Spirit in a foretaste of the heavenly liturgy. How does the Church do this?

... not only by celebrating the Eucharist, but also in other ways, especially by praying the Divine Office ... It is truly the voice of the bride addressing her bridegroom; it is the very prayer which Christ himself, together with his body, addresses to the Father ... Hence, all who perform this service are not only fulfilling a duty of the Church but also are sharing in the great honour accorded to Christ's spouse, for by offering these praises to God, they are standing before God's throne in the name of the Church. (SC 83, 84, 85)

Specifically, we remember, we praise and we give thanks, and these then flow into petition. Through text, symbol and gesture, we proclaim the reality of the Paschal Mystery in the eucharist, in all the sacraments and in the celebration of the Hours.

The psalms

The psalms form a major part of the prayer of the Church and so knowing how to pray them is vital. They reflect the whole range of our experiences and moods. As the General Instruction says, they express the pain and hope, misery and confidence of people of any age and land. (GILH 107)

The psalms are prayer – inspired by the Holy Spirit who is

141

> present with his grace to those believing Christians who, with good intention, sing and recite these songs. (GILH 100)

> The Spirit who inspired the psalmists is with us and in us, moving our hearts and minds, so we must be willing to be taught by him when we pray them. (GILH 104)

In spite of the eloquent recommendations given to them in the documents, anyone who has looked at the psalms will know that they present many difficulties to the Christian who takes them up for prayer. They need to be studied a little.

Firstly, the psalms are translated from the Hebrew. They present Hebrew culture and imagery. They are in poetic form, which is only partly evident in any modern language. There is a rhythm of meaning called parallelism, so that in any single verse the thought of the second line is parallel to, or echoes, the first, e.g. 'Day unto day takes up the story, night unto night shows forth the message' (Psalm 18(19)); 'O praise the Lord all you nations, acclaim him all you peoples' (Psalm 116(117)). Once we recognize this, we can appreciate the thought patterns of any psalm. Any good commentary on the psalms offers a full analysis of the different types of parallelism.

The second characteristic of Hebrew poetry is its metre, the alternation of strong and weak beats. This is lost in translation, although attempts have been made to retain the metre, for instance in the Gelineau psalms (Grail translation). We often think of the psalms as poems written by and for the individual, but this is not the case. They were written for the liturgy which was celebrated in the temple of Jerusalem. Even those psalms which express the emotions of an individual were used in Israel's liturgy. As in the entire Liturgy of the Hours, the psalms are vehicles of private prayer best expressed in common so that the individual details are subsumed by the rhythm of prayer and the opportunity to pray. It is through the language of the psalms that we learn the language of prayer.

The *New Jerome Biblical Commentary* suggests different types of psalms and groups them as follows:

- Hymns of praise (praising or blessing Yahweh);
- Hymns of lament (a prayer for help and deliverance, e.g. 'Hear ...', etc.);
- Royal psalms (in which the king is the speaker);
- Wisdom psalms (connected in some way with Old Testament wisdom literature);
- Liturgical psalms (deriving directly from Hebrew worship, especially from entrance processions into the temple);

- Historical psalms (recounting God's great works in the history of Israel).

Again, if we are able to distinguish the above categories when praying the psalms, we are better able to identify with them.

The content and structure of Morning and Evening Prayer[6]

Morning Prayer	Evening Prayer

INTRODUCTION

V *Lord, open our lips.*	V *O God, come to our aid.*
R *And we shall praise your name.*	R *O Lord, make haste to help us.*
[Invitatory psalm (Psalms 94(95), 99(100), 66(67) or 23(24)) with its antiphon]	*Glory be . . .*

HYMN

PSALMODY

A 'morning' psalm	A psalm
Old Testament Canticle	A psalm
A psalm of praise	New Testament Canticle

SCRIPTURE READING

(Silent Prayer)

SHORT RESPONSORY

GOSPEL CANTICLE

Benedictus	Magnificat

INTERCESSIONS

Consecrating the day to God	Intercession for the needs of the world

The Lord's Prayer

CONCLUDING PRAYER

BLESSING

143

Before briefly considering Morning and Evening Prayer, we must examine the elements common to all the hours which form their basic content.

The *opening hymn*: after an introductory verse, a hymn is sung. This gathers the people together as a community, provides a fitting introduction to the hour and helps to highlight the time of day, the feast and/or the season. We should not forget the great hymnodic tradition begun by the Fathers, e.g. 'Creator of the stars of night'. In the book, a hymn is indicated which is best sung; an appropriate alternative may be chosen and in private recitation a poem may be read.

The *psalms* form the major part of the Liturgy of the Hours. The compilers of the Hours were certainly aware of the difficulty some people experience with the psalms and have therefore included practical helps. Each psalm has a title indicating the general content and the literal meaning of the psalm. Antiphons are placed at the beginning and end of each one, pinpointing an important aspect; frequently they are quotations from the psalms themselves, which are now distributed over a four-week cycle. It is recommended that a psalm-prayer is said after the psalm to give a Christological perspective to it.

Canticles: Morning and Evening Prayer include a canticle from the Old and New Testaments respectively. Of their nature, psalms and canticles are songs and should be sung.

Extracts from Scripture are fairly short and are taken from the Old Testament and New Testament, except the gospels. In the Office of Readings, there are longer readings including one from non-biblical sources.

A brief response, the *responsory*, follows the reading, highlighting its meaning and applying it to the present. This may be omitted if it is not sung and where silent reflection would be more appropriate.

Intercessions occur in both Morning and Evening Prayer; in the morning they express the element of offering the day to God, in the evening the intercessions are concerned with the needs of the Church and the world. Since the early centuries the balance between praise and prayer has been integral to the Office. The intercessions at Morning and Evening Prayer are followed by the Lord's Prayer said by all present. Finally, there is a concluding prayer which corresponds to the Hour, the feast or the season being celebrated. Then there is a blessing and dismissal in the Morning and Evening and a brief conclusion at the other Hours: 'Let us bless the Lord – Thanks be to God.'

'Morning Prayer is the first of the two pivotal hours' of the day (Second Vatican Council). It is a way of sanctifying the morning. It speaks of new beginnings, light, day, work; Christ's resurrection is called to mind. We express unconditional praise of God in a meditative way. The scale of this celebration should be kept simple; in a parish, the number of people present will be relatively few, and the content of the hour may be adapted and abbreviated. A shortened form might include: a time to gather; a call to prayer; Psalm 94(95), known as the invitatory psalm; a thanksgiving prayer; a psalm of praise; the reading; intercessions; and a conclusion. A candle and a container with holy water might provide visual helps to prayer.

Evening Prayer, the second pivotal Hour, is a prayer of thanksgiving, repentance and petition. We welcome and praise Christ our light and ask his mercy and help. A 'cathedral' or parish celebration would be as follows: the service of light (lucernarium); the offering of incense in a call for mercy with evening Psalm 140(141); Scripture reading; intercessions; conclusion. These are sufficient elements for an adapted Evening Prayer of reasonable length and simplicity.

Ideally, the lucernarium begins in a darkened church or room into which the lighted Paschal candle or similar candle is brought by the presider. The candle is placed in its stand and a hymn to Christ our Light is sung. Alternatively, the candle is already in place and alight as the celebration begins. Smaller candles or nightlights might be arranged in different parts of the church and lit from the Paschal candle. Then a prayer of thanksgiving for the light follows. It is good to pause at the end of this prayer which concludes the service of light, to let the symbolism and silence speak for themselves. Then in silence, incense is added to prepared charcoal and Psalm 140(141) is sung. Again, a time of silence is recommended at the conclusion of the psalm, a time for reflection on the symbolism and the psalm. The psalm collect sums up the ritual action and the prayer. Then follow the reading and intercessions which may be formal or spontaneous. They lead into the Lord's Prayer and a concluding blessing.

From the late 1970s published examples of simplified Morning and Evening Prayer began to appear, beginning with GIA's *Praise God in Song* (1979) which gave settings compiled for interdenominational congregations at Notre Dame University. Paul Inwood's *Evening Prayer* (1983) was on the same lines, also *Holden Evening Prayer* (Marty Haugen). American hymnbooks (*Worship*, *Gather* and *Breaking Bread*) include such services as a matter of course and in Britain the first to do so was *New Songs of Celebration* (part of the *Complete Celebration Hymnal*). Guidelines were published in *Morning and Evening Prayer* (Liturgical Training Publications, Chicago). ICEL has prepared a resource book in 1993 and there have also been initiatives from the Anglicans and Catholics in England. These should provide a good supply both of prepared celebrations and of ideas which parish groups can gradually introduce into celebrations of their own compiling, adapted to their needs.

Conclusion

The final section of this chapter is a practical one. There are many pressing questions: How and when does a community get started? How much should be sung? How can one use symbols? Who presides? What other ministries are involved? How does one use the environment? and so forth. All these areas apply to Morning and Evening Prayer as printed in *The Prayer of the Church*, as well as to adapted forms as described above. Some parishes have started to develop a 'cathedral' type of Evening Prayer. It is hoped that this will become widely experienced and appreciated. The keynote throughout should be simplicity and flexibility.

Both Morning and Evening celebrations should have a format that can be easily and quickly memorized by all present. The hymn, psalm, and psalm refrain where this is used, should remain the same for the duration of the liturgical season in progress. Repetition and simplicity enable everyone present to participate fully without papers or books. Simplicity of structure, genuine symbols, silence, space and ritual gesture all contribute powerfully to real, heartfelt prayer. A parish might begin with Evening Prayer during Advent, Lent or Eastertime, or on the patronal feast of the parish. Another occasion might be in the context of a funeral; the revised Order of Christian Funerals strongly recommends Morning and Evening Prayer for the deceased. Whatever occasion gives rise to the introduction of the Prayer of the Church, take it, encourage and develop it. There is a need for non-eucharistic prayer in our parishes, prayer which is liturgical, involves ritual and symbol and is celebrated in common with either clergy or laity or, ideally, with both.

Music is an integral part of any liturgy and some singing should be introduced right from the start, with the hymn. Later, the group could sing the psalm or the psalm refrain and the gospel canticles, the Benedictus and Magnificat. The choice of hymn will depend on the time of day and the feast or season; it should not be chosen at random, but with regard to its content. The evening symbols of light and incense have been described above. For the morning, water, the cross, the bible, an icon, the rising sun are symbols which come to mind. Again, it is not quantity but quality and simplicity which help to create a prayerful atmosphere.

The ministries of a presider, an assistant, a reader and a psalmist or cantor are needed. Musicians are a help, but they are not essential. Nor is this a liturgy which requires a member of the clergy to preside;

any member of the group able to lead the community in prayer may undertake this. An assistant to the presider at Evening Prayer may carry the candles, give any directions needed and be of help to the presider. The cantor would lead the group in the psalm, if possible; there are different ways of reciting the psalm when it cannot be sung. Especially when starting, it is better to keep the number of ministers small; later, with an enlarged group, an acolyte or thurifer might be added. People are not invited to be presider or any other minister in order to be 'given a chance', but in the light of their individual gifts as leader, reader or cantor. Nor is any ministry a reward for good behaviour.

The setting for Morning and Evening Prayer needs careful thought in matters of space and lighting, the size of the area to be used and the focal point. It is preferable for the group to gather together in a comparatively small space, rather than facing the altar (the focus for the celebration of the eucharist). In this, as in many of the above suggestions, the group will experiment and discover from experience what is best for them and for the size of the group, taking into account the need for some movement and gesture.

The celebration of the Hours is a liturgy in its own right and should therefore be independent of any other devotion or liturgy, such as Benediction or Holy Hour with the Blessed Sacrament exposed, or the eucharist. Nevertheless, part of an hour might well be recited at a parish meeting or on another occasion. Weekday morning prayer may take place in the absence of a priest to say Mass. Whether holy communion is distributed during the course of the hour or not, is outside the scope of this chapter. Either way, the matter requires careful reflection and preparation. In many parts of the world a supply of consecrated hosts is not available, or obtainable only at great distance.

The reader may have many more queries such as where to find psalm tones, thanksgiving prayers and more. I would advise you to begin by keeping everything simple and direct. Gradually you will discern, with the group, what additions or refinements are possible. A prayerful celebration is all that is needed.

NOTES

1 Tessa Sheaf, 'Finding God in all things', *Intercom* (Catholic Communications Institute of Ireland, Dublin), vol. 22, no. 5 (June 1992), pp. 20–1.
2 G. J. Cuming, 'The New Testament foundation for common prayer', *Studia Liturgica* (1974), p. 91.
3 The term 'Cathedral Office' was coined by Anton Baumstark (1872–1948) to distinguish this prayer of the assembled people of God, the *ecclesia*, from the prayer of the monk. See his *Comparative Liturgy* (1948), and George Guiver, *Company of Voices* (London: SPCK, 1988), Part II, 'The history of daily prayer', pp. 49–146.

CELEBRATION: THE LITURGY HANDBOOK

4 See Eusebius, *Commentaries on the Psalms*; Gregory of Nyssa, *Life of St Macrina*, etc.
5 Robert Taft sj, *Beyond East and West* (Washington, DC: The Pastoral Press, 1984), p. 129.
6 From John Brook, *The School of Prayer: Introduction to the Divine Office for All Christians* (London: HarperCollins, 1992).

DOCUMENTATION AND BIBLIOGRAPHY

Articles in *Liturgy*, vol. 5, no. 1 (October 1980); vol. 13, nos 4 (April 1989) and 5 (June 1989).
General Instruction on the Liturgy of the Hours (GILH). Recommended version: *The Liturgy of the Hours*, ed. with a commentary by A.-M. Roguet op (London: Geoffrey Chapman, 1971; out of print).
J. D. Crichton, *Christian Celebration: Understanding the Prayer of the Church* (new edition; London: Geoffrey Chapman, 1993).
George Guiver, *Company of Voices: Daily Prayer and the People of God* (London: SPCK, 1988).
A. G. Martimort (ed.), *The Church at Prayer*, vol. IV (London: Geoffrey Chapman, 1986), pp. 151–275.
Robert Taft, *The Liturgy of the Hours in East and West* (Collegeville, MN: The Liturgical Press, 1986). Detailed and scholarly.
D. A. Withey, *Catholic Worship* (Bury St Edmunds: Kevin Mayhew, 1990), ch. 13.

148

Unit 9

J. D. CRICHTON

RITES OF COMMITMENT: MARRIAGE, THE SACRAMENT OF ORDERS

I. Marriage

> Marriage is a covenant in which a man and a woman set up a life-long bond with each other. This covenant draws its force and strength from creation. For Christians, however, it has been given an even higher dignity as one of the sacraments of the new covenant. (Order of Christian Marriage (1990), 1)

Marriage is one of the 'rites of passage' that are as old as the human race. As birth and death were surrounded with rites and ceremonies, so was marriage. These gave meaning and order to the great events of human existence and involved the whole community. Marriage, like the others, was a public event because the good of the community was seen to depend on it. Whether consciously or unconsciously, Church and State have continued, in different ways, to be concerned about marriage. It often comes as a shock to the young, and sometimes the not so young, to learn as they approach marriage that this is so. Marriage is inevitably a public event and, if only on account of its consequences (the family), society must be interested, indeed concerned, about it. In short, it is a social institution. Marriage is also as old as the human race (see Genesis 2:21–24; cf. Mark 10:7–9). It is a profoundly human institution but, as the OCM says (and indeed it is the common teaching of the Church), marriage has been raised by

149

Christ to the dignity of a sacrament. We now have to explore the meaning of that statement.

If we examine the documents of the Church (the Constitution on the Church in the Modern World, 47–52) and the texts of the Order of Christian Marriage, we find that the sacramental theology of marriage is built on three foundations: love, covenant and contract.

Love

It is not too much to say that in the last six decades the Church has rehabilitated the meaning of human love and has shown us the overriding importance of love (*caritas, agapē*) in the life of the Church and in the life of every Christian. Love is self-giving and not getting, and marriage is the great exemplar of human love. This is set out eloquently in one of the Prefaces of the Wedding Mass:

> You [God] created all of us to share your divine life.
> We see the high destiny of the human race in the love of
>   husband for wife,
> which bears the imprint of your own divine love.
> Love is our origin,
> Love is our constant calling,
> love is our fulfilment in heaven.
> The love of man and woman
> is made holy in the sacrament of marriage
> and becomes the mirror of your everlasting joy.
> For this we praise and thank God.

There is much that might be said about this text but we can only note here that in the sacrament of marriage human love is 'made holy' and thus bears the imprint of God's love. God's love is present (and active) in the love that husband and wife have for each other, so that we can say that they love each other with a love that is God's love communicated to them.

Covenant

It is noteworthy that whereas the older documents regularly spoke of marriage as a contract, the Constitution on the Church in the Modern Word and the Pastoral Instruction attached to the OCM almost always speak of marriage as a covenant (cf. OCM 1, 5, 6, 7). Marriage is thus put against the vast background of the covenant of the Old and New Testaments. There is revealed God's faithful love for the human race. He was (and is) always faithful to his promises to rescue, redeem, save his people. This faithful love reached its highest expression in the obedience of Jesus Christ to his Father when he gave himself for the redemption of the human race and brought into existence the new people of God, the Church which is his bride. Of this bridal Church marriage is the sacrament/sign which communicates to bride and bridegroom the covenantal love of Jesus Christ. Much of this is summed up in yet another Preface (II) of the Wedding Mass, in which we thank God through Jesus Christ our Lord who 'entered into a new covenant with your people ... This outpouring of love in the new covenant is symbolised in the marriage covenant that seals the love of husband and wife and reflects the divine plan of love.' Against this background Christian marriage stands out clearly as the mystery/sacrament/sign of the union between Christ and his Church.

This reminds us of Ephesians 5:21–33 which forms one of the possible readings at the Wedding Mass. But it needs to be put in context. The chapter begins: 'Try, then, to imitate God, as children of his that he loves, and follow Christ *by loving as he loved you*, giving himself up in our place as a fragrant offering and a sacrifice to God' (my italics). Self-giving, which is of the essence of married love, is sacrificial, as every married person knows. However difficult it may be to sustain it, such a love is possible since it is strengthened and transfused by the love of Christ who gave himself for us in his passion, death and resurrection; it is Christ's love that is communicated to husband and wife through the sacrament, not only on their wedding day but throughout their lives. Because marriage is a sacrament it is a participation in the Paschal Mystery. As the OCM says, 'As once God encountered his people in a covenant of love and faithfulness, so now the Saviour of the human race presents himself as the bridegroom of the Church and fulfils his covenant with her in his paschal mystery' (6; and see Constitution on the Church in the Modern World, 48).

This self-sacrificial love is expressed and declared in the words of the consent which, with slight modifications, have been used in this country for seven hundred years:

> I take you
> to be my wedded wife/husband,
> to have and to hold
> from this day forward;
> for better, for worse,
> for richer, for poorer,
> in sickness and in health,
> to love and to cherish
> till death us do part;
> and this do I pledge with my vow.

Nothing could be more explicit, and it is difficult to think of anything more inclusive. Husband and wife take each other and love each other *whatever* may come; poverty or riches, sickness or health and all the circumstances of married life are so many ways whereby husband and wife love each other until death shall part them. Divorce is ruled out.

The same text points up another important feature of Christian marriage. It is a permanent sacrament and husband and wife celebrate and live the sacrament day by day. It, or rather they, are a living sacrament which does not take place in a few hours on the wedding day but occupies their whole lives. Thus doing, or striving to do,

> they show forth and share in the mystery and fruitful love which exists between Christ and the Church. Accordingly they help each other to grow in holiness, both in their married life and in welcoming and rearing children. Among the people of God they have a special place and enjoy a special gift (*charisma*). (OCM 8; and see Constitution on the Church, 11)

They bear witness to Christ and his love in their domestic life, not only to each other and their children, but also to the society in which they live: 'As they celebrate the mystery of Christ united with his Church, he enriches their marriage and they receive grace to live rightly as faithful witnesses of the Lord' (OCM 11). Or as another text puts it more concretely, when a couple celebrate their marriage (and one would add, when they live it) 'they offer a visible and effective sign of God's faithful love and presence to the community . . . and to the whole people of God' (OCM 40).

Contract

As has been observed above, the Order of Christian Marriage speaks of the sacrament as a covenant. We find the word contract in the Code of Canon Law, Canon 1055/2, though in Canon 1057 it calls marriage an 'irrevocable covenant'. But if the word does not occur, the reality does and the young (and others too) are put off when they hear that marriage is a contract and a binding contract at that. Yet it is common enough and is found in the ordination service when the ordinand undertakes lifelong celibacy and when a religious makes his or her solemn profession. Not only is the contract entered into but there is an external sign: a written document, signed by the candidate. In the rite of marriage, contract ensures that the spouses are entering freely into the covenant, for without freedom there is no contract of any kind. Contract is then the formal expression of this truth and is enshrined in the questions that take place at the beginning of the celebration.

So far nothing has been said about the 'ends of marriage' which, since St Augustine, have been called the 'goods' of marriage. These are union (two in one flesh), children and fidelity. It is to these presumably that the Constitution on the Liturgy (77) refers when it says that the marriage rite must be revised so that the grace of the sacrament may be more clearly signified and 'the duties of the spouses impressed upon them'. But it should not be thought that 'the duties' are imposed by 'the Church', understood as the clergy. The ends of marriage are implied in its very nature and emerge from it. The great grace of marriage is that it makes two people as one – two in one flesh – though each retains her/his personhood and dignity. As the documents say, it is a *consortium*, a living together of two equal persons. From this unique union come children, the fruit of the union and its most conspicuous sign. Fidelity is the necessary consequence of the marriage union that is exclusive 'of any other', exclusive of the sin called adultery. All these find expression in different places in the marriage rite.

The Liturgy of Marriage

With the Order of Christian Marriage of 1969 came the first revision of the rite since 1614, though England had always retained its own rite, substantially that of the Sarum *Manuale* of the Middle Ages. In 1990 there was a further revision of the Roman rite, one notable feature of which is the invocation of the Holy Spirit in the texts of the nuptial blessing. The *Praenotanda* (Pastoral Instruction) have been increased from 18 to 44, giving an extended liturgico-pastoral theology of marriage which has been drawn on in the first part of this chapter.

Both editions of the rite of marriage, however, allowed for the adaptation and addition to the Roman Rite (see OCM 39, 40 and the Constitution on the Liturgy, 37–40). For some years now the national Pastoral Rites Committee of England and Wales has been working on a revised rite for those countries. An important description of the proposed rite (or rather rites) is to be found in *Priests and People* (July 1992), pp. 269–74. In what follows I shall be basing my remarks on this rite, though I must emphasize that at the time of writing it has to be approved by the Conference of Bishops and confirmed by Rome. It is *not authorized for use*.

As has been said above, the sacrament of marriage is not confined to its liturgical celebration. It is a sacrament that is lived throughout the years and needs preparation beforehand. This is true of Christian initiation (baptism, confirmation and eucharist) and, as we have learned, the catechumenate can last a very long time. It is this understanding of sacramental celebration and the experience that has gone with it that is represented in the proposed Liturgy of Marriage.

One of the oldest elements of the marriage liturgy was betrothal. It was known to the Jews (Matthew 1:18) and the (pagan) Romans and continued throughout the Middle Ages. It seems to have been a domestic rite (though the clergy might be present) when the future partners pronounced the *verba de futuro*, words promising that the couple intended to enter into marriage. The counterpart to this in more modern times was engagement, which was almost always a secular event. Two young people exchanged rings, perhaps in the course of a family party. In our own time this seems to have disappeared or become a purely private affair between the two concerned. There are even less desirable practices about which nothing will be said here. However, it has been clear for a long time that since marriage is for life it requires preparation, and nowadays there is some considerable time between the announcement of a marriage and its celebration. The proposed liturgy suggests that this period should be precisely a time of preparation, for which simple rites are provided, to take place either at home or in church. They are sharply and necessarily distinguished from marital consent but they do make provision for a period that covers instruction, prayer and reflection. It is conceived as a first step towards the great undertaking of marriage.

The proposed liturgy then deals with the rite of marriage itself, which will be considered below. After this it provides simple but very adequate rites (texts and prayer) for the celebration of anniversaries (25 and 50 years) and reconciliations. These may take place either at home or in church with the eucharist. (There are also 'Rites and Pastoral Notes for Particular Circumstances', e.g. marriage between a Christian and a non-Christian, which we cannot consider here.)

The compilers of this proposed Liturgy of Marriage take the Wedding Mass as the typical rite, rightly in the opinion of the present writer. It is here that the depth and breadth of the meaning of marriage are given and it is a matter of experience that when celebrated with care and dignity it makes a profound impression on all present, including the bride and bridegroom. The rite of the Mass is familiar; so only those features of the marriage rite that are new will be commented on here. It should be borne in mind, however, that the changes are *proposals* and are not (yet) part of the rite.

The entrance rite

It has long been felt that the beginning of our present marriage rite is cumbersome and appears almost as a duplication of the exchange of promises. It is proposed then that a revised rite, involving declarations of freedom to marry and intent to do so, shall take place in the porch of the church. The procession then follows. (If there are difficulties about this, the rite is transferred to the beginning of the marriage rite proper after the homily.) To the declarations of the couple a response by the gathered assembly is provided.

The Mass begins with the opening prayer, and the readings with psalm and Alleluia continue in the usual way.

The marriage rite proper

After the homily the minister gathers the bride and bridegroom and their assistants before the sanctuary and asks the couple to exchange their promises. This they do in the traditional words, now put in the second person plural (you) and with one phrase added. The minister ratifies their consent in a short statement that includes the words 'What God has joined together, let no one put asunder'.

At this point the Order provides an acclamation to be sung (said) by the whole assembly. It is in the form of a Jewish blessing prayer, 'Blessed are you, heavenly Father . . .'. The signing of the registers now takes place in full view of the assembly.

Since the nuptial blessing is so directly related to the essence of marriage it is suggested, following a German precedent, that it should take place at this point, though the other position after the Lord's Prayer is still allowed.

The nuptial blessing

The prayer known as the nuptial blessing is a high point in the celebration and communicates the depths of the meaning of Christian marriage. In the Roman Order there are three prayers; in the proposed English Order others have been composed. Lack of space prohibits commentary. All one would say is that they might well be pondered on during the time of preparation before marriage. One feature, however, may be noted. It has long been felt that in the text of the ancient nuptial blessing (sixth century) there should be inserted an invocation of the Holy Spirit and this has been done in the three prayers of the Roman Order and, of course, in the English prayers. Thus we find in Blessing I:

> Look with love on this couple
> now joined to each other in marriage.
> They ask your blessing.
> Send the grace of the Holy Spirit upon them,
> that your love may fill their hearts
> and they may remain faithful in the covenant of marriage.

Since the nuptial blessing has the nature of a eucharistic prayer (in a broad sense), the English authors have composed prayers based on the pattern of *thanksgiving*, *anamnesis* (calling to mind) and *epiclesis* (invocation of the Holy Spirit).

If the nuptial blessing takes place after the consents, what are called the 'illustrative rituals' are now separated from them, thus showing their subordinate role in the liturgy. These are the prayers over the rings (and/or the couple) and the exchange of gifts, the old Sarum element that is now brought back into the rite. The local parish community may also present the couple with a gift.

There is little need to say anything about the Liturgy of the Eucharist, but we may note one or two matters. It is important that there should be a procession to present the bread and wine and if this cannot be conveniently done by the bride and bridegroom it should be done by the members of their respective families. It is one of the oldest processions of the Roman Rite and should not be neglected, whatever the practical difficulties. It is also urged that even if it is not the custom of the parish, holy communion should be given in both kinds (cf. references to the wedding feast of Cana in various texts of the rite).

To sum up the importance of the celebration of marriage we may borrow an injunction of the OCM. Pastors are to see that the celebration of marriage is *pastorally effective*, clearly expressing that the couple are showing forth the union and fruitful love between Christ and his Church and participating in this mystery (14/3; emphasis mine).

Consistent with their belief that the celebration of marriage is a 'journey', the compilers provide 'domestic rites' for use after the wedding. First, there are prayers of blessing, from various sources, over food and drink which may be used at the 'wedding breakfast' (it is now often a very late lunch) or later on. Secondly, there is a rite for the blessing of a new home (with or without a Mass) which is a real service with prayers, readings and, of course, blessing. Notable is a special blessing over the newly married couple.

In addition, and looking further ahead, the Order provides rites (to be used within or outside Mass) for anniversaries (twenty-fifth and fiftieth). Finally, there is a rite for family reconciliation in the home when there have been difficulties, tensions or animosity. This is a most valuable contribution to the living of marriage which, as everyone knows, is fraught with problems from time to time.

The long second half of the Order contains 'Rites and Pastoral Notes for Particular Circumstances' which range from the marriages of those who do not practise regularly to a marriage with a non-believer and inter-church marriages. Pastorally speaking, the suggestions and material provided are very necessary and they are in line with the need in these and similar circumstances for adaptation.

Pastoral considerations

The greater part of the OCM is taken up with what might be called pastoral advice directed to the clergy, to those getting married and to the local parish community generally.

Understandably, much emphasis is laid on the need for adequate preparation for marriage; as marriages are now usually planned long before the event, there is plenty of time for such preparation. The basis of this instruction is to be found in the first eleven paragraphs of the OCM (see 17) and the sessions should include prayer and an examination of the texts of the rite and the content of the Scripture readings to be used. Lay people may take part in this process of preparation (OCM 26) and this can be a very valuable help.

There can of course be awkward situations and OCM, following the teaching of Pope John Paul's *Familiaris Consortio*, states that faith (even faint) is required for marriage in church and if the couple reject 'what the Church intends when celebrating marriage' they are to be told that their marriage cannot take place in church (OCM 21). Recourse to the competent authority may be necessary and is anyway the prudent thing to do. There are other circumstances, less dramatic, when a Wedding Mass is contra-indicated. The partners may not have practised for some years, their friends and acquaintances may be non-Catholics or even non-Christians. The OCM suggests (29) that in these circumstances the Mass should be omitted.

Several times the OCM insists that the celebration of marriage is an event that concerns the whole of the local community. See for instance 29: 'Since marriage is intended to increase and sanctify the people of God, its celebration is communal and calls for the participation of the people.' Too often marriage is regarded as a private affair between the couple and their relatives. But according to OCM the *parish* should be invited to the liturgical celebration and make their contribution to the singing and praying; as the Constitution on the Liturgy laid down, all liturgical services are celebrations of the Church, including of course the local community (SC 7, 14, 28). The celebration is greatly enhanced and indeed facilitated when it is supported by members of the parish community. With such participation better-quality music can be chosen and all the singing can be more effective. The proposed rite for England and Wales provides opportunities for other forms of participation by the parish community.[1]

By way of conclusion I take the liberty of quoting a whole paragraph from the proposed English/Welsh Order. It gives the rationale of the liturgy and sums up so much of what the celebration of marriage is:

The sacrament of marriage is a lifelong covenant, whose

celebration should not be restricted to the wedding service. In earlier centuries, our forebears marked with liturgical rites not just the exchange of consent but also the betrothal and the entry into the marital home. In the circumstances of our time, in which the very institution of marriage is threatened by so many pressures, the importance of thoroughgoing preparation and of ongoing support and help for marriage is universally recognized. Moreover, the Church's recent experience with the initiation of adults has demonstrated the potential of an integrated spiritual, catechetical, and liturgical formation for individuals preparing for life long commitment, as well as the value of phasing the celebration of such sacramental commitment over a number of stages. (37)

NOTE

1 It seems odd that people should so often be *married* and *buried* to the dismal tones of 'Crimond', 'The Lord's my shepherd'.

DOCUMENTATION AND BIBLIOGRAPHY

Ordo Celebrandi Matrimonium (2nd *editio typica*, 1990). In course of translation.

For the proposed English/Welsh rite see *Liturgy*, vol. 10, no. 5 (June 1986), vol. 11, no. 4 (April 1987).

J. D. Crichton, *Christian Celebration: Understanding the Sacraments* (new edition; London: Geoffrey Chapman, 1993), pp. 116–37.

Christopher Walsh, 'Revising the Rites of Marriage', *Priests and People*, vol. 6, no. 7 (July 1992), pp. 269–74. A most useful summary and commentary on the proposed English/Welsh rite of marriage.

II. The sacrament of orders

It might seem that the revision of the rites of ordination is not a matter that deeply concerns the laity. A priest is appointed to a parish, he appears at the altar and the people assume he is duly authorized, i.e. ordained. They may ask 'What's his name?' But the question is not *who* he is but *what* he is. What has ordination made him?

As for the bishop, he is an Important Person, he comes to a parish to administer confirmation, he appears occasionally for other purposes and it is a matter of general though rather vague knowledge that he ordains priests – oh, and yes, deacons. But how was the bishop made a bishop and what, after all, is he? Then there are those deacons, some of them now called 'permanent', but how does a deacon differ from a priest?

These questions can be answered by reading a manual of theology but they are also answered by the liturgy of ordination with its various rites. For the *lex orandi* is the *lex credendi* (what is celebrated in the liturgy teaches us what to believe). This teaching has been made very much clearer by the revision of the liturgy of ordination which in the Middle Ages had been cluttered up with a number of secondary rites. If the liturgy was to deliver its message certain clarifications were necessary and these began to come before the Second Vatican Council. Pius XII in 1947, thanks to the studies of scholars, was able to state authoritatively that the laying-on of hands with prayer was the essential rite of ordination whether of a bishop, a priest or a deacon. Vatican II for its part firmly established that the episcopate is the primary participation in the one priesthood of the Church, that of Jesus Christ, so that the bishop is sacramentally at the apex of Holy Order.

Here are two of the Council's statements (LG 21):

> In Bishops ... for whom priests are assistants, our Lord Jesus Christ, the supreme High Priest, is present in the midst of those who believe ... They are shepherds of the Lord's flock, they are servants of Christ, stewards of the mysteries of Christ and witnesses to the ministration of the Spirit to make men just.

> For the discharging of such great duties the apostles were enriched by Christ with a special outpouring of the Holy Spirit ... This spiritual gift they passed on to their helpers by the imposition of hands ... and by episcopal consecration is conferred *the fullness of the sacrament of orders* (which) is called the high priesthood, the apex of the sacred ministry.

This teaching puts an end to an ancient dispute whether the episcopate was simply an office of jurisdiction and administration.

The Council also made clear that ordination is the inclusion of a person in a corporate body, the *ordo*, to which he belongs and with whose members he collaborates in the work of the Church not only in his own diocese but with the Pope in the work of the Church throughout the world. As was seen very clearly in the early centuries of the Church, *communio*, the union of the Church, was maintained precisely by the relationships which the bishops had with one another. This *communio* was expressed liturgically by the inclusion of the name of the Pope or the Patriarch in the prayers of the eucharist. Withdrawal of the name spelt *ex*-communication.

The priestly Church

There is another strand in the teaching of Vatican II that was somewhat overshadowed in the past. The priest (including the bishop, of course) was said to be 'set apart' from the people – so much so that to some he seemed a different species of human being. One is reminded of the riposte of St Thomas More to people who were complaining of the misdeeds and poor quality of the contemporary clergy: 'They be from you', he said. Long before that, in the fourth century, St Augustine expressed his worries about being a bishop because it seemed to give him a certain *rank*: 'The care of my rank has always, for some reason I find hard to explain, worried me, I mean as to why this burden was placed on my shoulders' (Sermon 340) and it was in a similar context that he made the statement that has now become famous: 'For you I am a bishop; *with you* I am a Christian.'

The 'with you' is spelt out in another way by the Constitution on the Church and the Constitution on the Liturgy (14). Christ is the high priest of his body the Church and all baptized Christians share in his priesthood as was taught in the first letter of St Peter: 'Like living stones be yourselves built into a spiritual house, to be a holy priesthood, to offer spiritual sacrifices acceptable to God through Jesus Christ' (2:5, 9). From among the people certain men are chosen (and in the early Church the *people* chose them) to share in the priesthood of Christ, as bishops, as presbyters (priests) and deacons. But the basis of their ordination is baptism and in this they are Christians 'with' the people. Endowed, however, with a spiritual gift (*charisma*) they are appointed to serve the people by celebrating the liturgy with and for them, by teaching and by pastoral care. They are 'for' the people by ordination, 'con-corporate' with the people, as Vatican II also said, sharing their joys and their sorrows and being *with* them in all the vicissitudes of their life.

Ministry in the New Testament and the early Church

The data in the New Testament on Holy Orders are disparate and difficult to co-ordinate. The apostles chose certain officers (see Ephesians 2:19–22; 3:11) and appointed others to pastoral charges. Some of these were *episcopoi* and other presbyters; see, for example, 1 Timothy 3:1–7; 5:17 (presbyters). We also hear of bishops (*episcopoi*) and deacons in Philippians 1:1. Bishops at any rate were appointed by the laying-on of hands: 'You have in you a spiritual gift (*charisma*) which was given to you when the prophets spoke and the elders (presbyters) laid their hands on you' (1 Timothy 4:14). When Paul and Barnabas were sent on a mission there was prayer, fasting and a laying-on of hands (Acts 13:1–3). What is very clear by AD 96 is that as the apostles were sent by Christ so they sent others to be 'bishops and deacons' (*Letter of Clement to the Corinthians*, 42). In the letters of St Ignatius of Antioch (died *c.* 110) the threefold ministry is already in existence, at least in those churches of Asia Minor to which he wrote, though as yet this system may not have been found everywhere. From this we can gather that the bishop normally celebrated the eucharist, assisted by his deacon-servant and surrounded by his council, the presbyters. It was thus that Ignatius envisaged the local community, presided over by the bishop at a single altar. The Constitution on the Liturgy (41) recalls this picture and sees it as the sacrament-sign of the nature of the Church.

The first liturgy of ordination

The first liturgy of ordination is not found until the second decade of the third century, in a document called the *Apostolic Tradition*, generally regarded as having been written by Hippolytus, a Roman priest. It is of the greatest importance since all rites of ordination in the Church of both East and West derive from it. In it we find the threefold order of bishop, presbyter and deacon with their respective ordination prayers. Since the prayer for the bishop has been restored to use in the Roman Rite we will consider it lower down. But a few words about the ordination prayers for presbyter and deacon will be in place here. The ordaining bishop lays his *hand* on the candidate (for the presbyterate) and prays that God may give him 'the Spirit of grace and counsel so that he may rule and govern the people'. At this time it seems the presbyter had no specific liturgical function. The chief celebrant was the bishop, the presbyters stood in a half-circle around him, remaining silent during the eucharistic prayer. In the ordination of a deacon the bishop laid his *hands* on him but the text of the prayer makes clear that the deacon does not share in the 'seniority' of the presbyter – he does what the bishop tells him to do![1]

The subsequent history of the liturgy of ordination is long and complicated and we must now pass to the revised rite, which appeared first in 1968 and again with further revisions in 1990. This second edition, by the very arrangement of the texts (*first* the Ordination of a Bishop, secondly the Ordination of a Presbyter, and thirdly the Ordination of a Deacon) better expresses the theology of the Constitution on the Church (LG) referred to above.

The ordination of a bishop

The *rite* can be set out like this:

1. After the gospel and the singing of the *Veni, creator Spiritus*, the bishop-elect is presented to the consecrating bishop.
2. The homily of the consecrating bishop.
3. The interrogatory, i.e. the traditional questions about a bishop's obligations.
4. Prayer of the assembly in the form of the Litany of Saints.
5. The laying-on of hands by the consecrator in silence. The co-consecrators do likewise.
6. The placing of the Gospel Book on the elect's head.
7. The prayer of ordination.
8. The anointing of the elect's head with chrism.
9. He is given the insignia (ring, mitre and staff or crozier) and is handed the Gospel Book.
10. If consecrated in his own cathedral he is led to his chair (*cathedra*) by two of the consecrating bishops. The kiss of peace is exchanged.

The homily, which is not a fixed text of the rite, is interesting as it is by and large a summary of the teaching of Vatican II. We may note, however, the emphasis on the *charisma*, the gift given in ordination: bishops, successors of the apostles, receive the gift of the Holy Spirit by the imposition of hands and thereby also 'the fullness of the sacrament of Order'. We may also note that Christ the high priest is said to be *present* in the bishop (seen as surrounded by his council of presbyters) when he is proclaiming the Gospel, teaching the people and in his whole sacramental ministry. It is also interesting to note that the bishop is to have a special care for the poor, the oppressed, the stranger and the exile. For this, of course, he will need the co-operation of his presbyters and deacons, as also of the laity.

The questions put to a bishop-elect are traditional and used to be very lengthy and, of course, in Latin. They have been greatly shortened to everyone's relief, including no doubt the bishop-elect's. They ask that he shall work in collaboration with his fellow-bishops and in obedience to the Apostolic See, and for the rest they resume in question and answer form much that has been said (or may have been said) in the homily.

The prayer of ordination (or consecration) with the laying-on of hands is clearly the very heart of the whole rite. In this way bishops have been ordained from the early third century onwards and almost certainly earlier (the laying-on of hands is already a rite in the New Testament) and, as we have seen, the prayer is that of Hippolytus, author of the *Apostolic Tradition*. The prayer, though short, is full of meaning and deserves a lengthy commentary.[2] What must however be mentioned is what is regarded as the operative section, which is pronounced by all the consecrating bishops together:

> Pour out now on this your elect that strength (*virtutem*) which is from you, the *sovereign Spirit*, whom you gave to your beloved Son [child = servant] Jesus Christ, the Spirit he himself gave to the holy apostles who established the church in different places to the unceasing praise and glory of your name.

This is a brief but very meaningful statement: the sovereign, guiding, leading Spirit who came upon Jesus at his baptism and totally filled him in his resurrection, and was transmitted to the apostles who in turn handed it on to their followers, this Spirit is now given to the bishop who kneels before his consecrators.

On this basis the prayer makes clear the functions of the bishop: he is shepherd of the flock, he serves God by prayer and by 'offering the gifts of your holy church', i.e. by celebrating the eucharist. From the Holy Spirit and through Christ he receives the authority to forgive sins and it is his role to 'rule' the church given into his care, and that rule is to be gentle and fair-minded.

The other rites are intended to be 'explanatory', unfolding the meaning of the episcopate through symbols. The holding of the Gospel Book over the head of the elect is a very ancient rite, known in the fourth century in the Church of both East and West. It may signify the giving of the fullness of the Spirit and refer back to Luke 4:16–21 or it may mean that the bishop is to live under the yoke of the Gospel. The second, revised edition of the rite sees it as the sign of the bishop's duty to preach the Gospel. The anointing of the head signifies that the episcopate is the primary participation in the high priesthood of Christ; the putting-on of the ring is a symbol of the bishop's 'marriage' to his diocese (an ancient notion); the mitre is now seen as a sign that the bishop is to seek holiness of life; and the pastoral staff (crozier) obviously shows that the bishop is shepherd of the flock, as the prayer of consecration has said.

Ordination to the presbyterate (priesthood)

As said above, the rite follows the same order as that for the ordination of a bishop: the presentation of the candidate, the homily, the interrogatory (new), the Litany of Saints, the laying-on of hands, the ordination prayer, the explanatory rites (the anointing of the hands, the vesting, the offering of bread and wine brought by the people) and finally the kiss of peace.

As in the ordination of a bishop, the laying-on of hands with the ordination prayer stands out as the essential rite. All else is subsidiary, including the 'handing over' of the paten and chalice.

The homily, though only a specimen offered for the use of the ordaining bishop, is not without its importance. It summarizes a good deal of the Council documents on priesthood and states the nature of the order and the principal functions of the priest. Right at the beginning it states that the whole people of God is a 'royal priesthood' and, like the homily for the episcopate, that as Christ chose apostles and they chose their successors, so now men are chosen to be co-workers with the bishop and servants of the people of God. The priest is to be formed in the image of Christ by ordination, sharing thus in the priesthood of the bishop. The bond, then, between priest and bishop is not simply juridical but *sacramental*: both share in different degrees in the one priesthood of Christ.

As for his functions, the priest is ordained to preach the Word of God, to give pastoral care to the people committed to his charge and to celebrate 'the Lord's sacrifice'. But these must not be merely formal activities. The priest must meditate on the Scriptures, believe what he reads, teach what he believes and imitate in his life what he preaches. Even more deeply, Christ's sacrifice which he celebrates must be the pattern of his living. In the old phrase, he is to imitate (in his life) that which he handles at the altar. The ministry of the other sacraments, baptism, penance, and the anointing of the sick, are recalled and the candidate is exhorted to praise and thank God in the prayer of the Divine Office, for this also is a ministry not only for his people but also for the whole world.

Of the interrogatory that follows we need only say that the five answers of the candidate sum up the principal themes of the ordination rite and the meaning of the priesthood. Under the guidance of the Holy Spirit and as a co-worker with the bishop, the priest has a pastoral care of the people and a ministry of the Word and sacraments, especially the eucharist. Finally, he promises obedience to his bishop.

The prayer of ordination is ancient, going back at least to the sixth century and perhaps to the fifth (it has been attributed to St Leo the Great), and like any text as old as that it bears the marks of its age. In the 1990 edition it has been revised, to its advantage.

Two or three verbal changes apart, the content of the prayer is as follows. The *same* Spirit is given to both the bishop and the priest, who shares certain functions with the bishop. This reference to the (holy) Spirit leads to another, Numbers 11:16, 17, where we are told that at the behest of God Moses took some of the spirit given to him and put it on the seventy elders who were to help him in ruling the people.

The priestly order in the Old Testament was that of Aaron and his sons but its typology has always been a little difficult since the Christian priesthood derives from him who was the 'type' of Christ, namely Melchizedek. In the revised edition we read that Aaron and his sons were appointed to offer the sacrifices of the Tabernacle 'which were the foreshadowing of the good things to come' (Hebrews 8:5). This is followed by a quite new passage where we read that God in the appointed time sent his Son into the world (John 3:17); he is the Apostle and High Priest of our faith (Hebrews 3:1) who by the Holy Spirit offered himself to the Father, an unblemished sacrifice (Hebrews 9:14), and made his apostles, consecrated in truth (John 17:19), sharers in his mission. To them he added co-operators 'of the second order' (*comites*) to proclaim and celebrate the work of salvation throughout the world.

By these additions the prayer is greatly enriched. We note that the missionary element in priesthood is emphasized: priests are to see themselves as having a duty, alongside the bishop, to proclaim the Gospel to all.

To their duties as ministers of baptism and the eucharist are now explicitly added the sacrament of reconciliation and the sacraments of the sick. Like the bishop, the priest must pray for his people, but praying *with* them by using the Prayer of the Church is not mentioned.[3]

Of the explanatory rites the anointing of the hands is the most important. As the formula that accompanies the act shows, it is a 'consecration': 'May our Lord Jesus Christ whom the Father anointed with power and the Holy Spirit keep you that you may sanctify the Christian people and offer sacrifice to God.' This is the priest's liturgical function. The ministry of teaching and preaching the Word of God is emphasized in the ordination prayer and the preliminary questions.

In the old days when the anointing of the hands took place the *Veni, creator Spiritus* ('Come, Holy Ghost') was sung and everybody thought that the real business of ordination was now taking place. The revised Order has suppressed that hymn at this place and replaced it with Psalm 109(110), with its antiphon 'You are a priest for ever' – a much more comprehensible arrangement.

The second rite that calls for mention is the handing of the eucharistic bread and wine to the newly ordained. These are brought to the bishop by the *laity* and presented to the bishop first, who then hands them to the priest with the words: 'Receive the offering of the holy people which is to be offered to God. Realize what you are to do, imitate the mystery you are going to handle and conform your life to the mystery of the Lord's cross.' What the priest is, and what are his principal functions, is made very clear by the whole of the rite.

The kiss of peace which concludes the rite and the laying-on of the presbyters' hands before the ordination prayer are signs that the newly ordained is incorporated into the 'order of presbyters'.

In conclusion it can be said that the rite of ordination to the priesthood shows very clearly that the presbyter shares with the bishop the one priesthood of Christ, in whose name he preaches and celebrates. The work of the Church and the mission of the Church depend on both bishop and presbyter working in harmony for the building up of the Church until the end of time.

Ordination to the diaconate

The Second Vatican Council made two changes: the subdiaconate (a major order only since the thirteenth century) was suppressed and the permanent diaconate was restored and could be received by married men. For centuries the diaconate was no more than a stage on the way to the priesthood. This still remains, but alongside the permanent diaconate. To the former is now attached the obligation of celibacy, and a formal declaration of acceptance now has to be made before ordination to the bishop or his deputy. These changes have brought with them some small modifications of the rite.

The rite follows the pattern of the other two: the ordination takes place after the gospel and the homily, there is the interrogatory and the Litany of Saints. Then the bishop (only) lays hands on the candidate in silence and there follows the prayer of ordination. The candidate is then vested in dalmatic and stole and the bishop hands him the symbol of his office, the Book of the Gospels.

No doubt because the diaconate had for so long been no more than a stage on the way to priesthood the deacon's role is unclear. It is at least partly clarified by the homily and the ordination prayer.

From the former we can gather that he has a liturgical ministry: he assists the bishop (or priest) at the eucharist; he reads the gospel, prepares the offerings and gives communion (especially from the chalice). He baptizes, presides at marriages, takes communion to the sick and the dying and presides at funeral services (other than the Mass). It is also his function to teach and preach and to conduct non-liturgical services. So far, so clear.

The homily goes on to speak of the deacon's 'charitable' role, and it is here that uncertainty begins. It is true that in the early centuries of the Church deacons had the material care of large numbers of people, the widows, virgins, sick and poor whom the Church supported. This situation cannot be restored (though some great churches like

Westminster Cathedral are providing homes and night shelter for the homeless) but in the ever-increasing shortage of priests it would seem that permanent deacons might well be commissioned to *administer* parishes that are without resident clergy. What it comes to is that 'charity' is a very broad term. It could cover teaching, which is recommended as the work of the deacon; if he is properly equipped, he could do invaluable work among the young and those approaching the Church.

The ordination prayer is the old Roman prayer, which has undergone some revision. After an introduction, it speaks of the diversity in unity of the Church made up of many members but bonded together and made one by the Holy Spirit. This Spirit was active in the first days of the Church when, with prayer and the laying-on of hands, the apostles communicated the Spirit to the seven to be 'ministers of tables' (Acts 6:1–6). The ordaining bishop continues: 'Send forth your Spirit, Lord, on these servants that they may faithfully perform their office, strengthened by the sevenfold gift of your grace.' He then prays that they may be examples of evangelical virtue, filled with sincere love, having a care for the sick and the poor (i.e. the charitable work of the deacon) and, in their personal life, self-controlled and modest.

Since the same prayer is rightly used for 'ordinary' deacons who are committed to celibacy and for permanent deacons who are usually married, it was necessary to make a change towards the end of the prayer. For 'example of *chastity*' the text now reads 'example of behaviour' (*conversationis*). Purity has already been mentioned, so now the prayer can emphasize that it is the whole conduct of the deacon that is to be an example to others. The prayer ends appropriately with a reference to *service*: the deacon is to be like Christ who came not to be served but to serve (Mark 10:45).

The deacon is now vested with stole and dalmatic and the Book of the Gospels is handed to him with the words: 'Receive the Gospel of Christ whose herald you now are; believe what you read, teach what you believe and imitate (in your life) what you teach.' Meanwhile Psalm 145, which speaks of the service of the poor and sick, is sung, its message underlined by the antiphon: 'If anyone serves me, my Father who is in heaven will honour him.'

The lesser ministries

As early as the middle of the third century, 'minor orders' were known in Rome: doorkeeper, reader, exorcist and acolyte. In the course of time some of these became obsolete and all somewhat fossilized. They were so many steps to the subdiaconate (now suppressed), the diaconate and the priesthood. They were conferred on seminarians at various points in their training. Pope Paul VI in 1972 decided to suppress all except the offices of reader and acolyte. These offices may also be conferred on lay men, for they are conceived as ways of *serving the people*. Thus the reader, as well as having a function in church, may 'instruct the faithful in the worthy reception of the sacraments' and, if capable, train others for the function of reading in the liturgy.

Neither the reader nor the acolyte is 'ordained'. Like similar officers in the third century, they are appointed. The rite is quite simple: after the Liturgy of the Word in the eucharist, or at the end of a similar liturgy without the eucharist, the candidate comes before the celebrant, who invites the assembly to pray and then recites a prayer by which the candidate is blessed. Then he is handed a Bible with the charge to read it and hand on to others the Word of God.

The acolyte is appointed for the service of the altar, assisting the priest or deacon at the eucharist. But he may also give communion to the sick, instruct those who serve at the altar, and expose the Blessed Sacrament but not give the blessing. The rite is the same as for the reader except that the sign of office given to him is a vessel containing bread and wine.

It may be thought that these ministries are nowadays hardly necessary. Lay people, both men and women, have been exercising the office of reader for twenty-five years, and men and boys have been altar servers for time out of mind. However, readers, formally appointed after adequate training in the Scriptures and their proclamation, could be of great assistance in parishes. They could not only train others but could preside at services of the Word (like the Divine Office) and be on hand for baptisms, marriages and funerals. Indeed, if the reader has the necessary ability and training, he may act as cantor and would be very useful in assisting at the above services.

A formal ministry in parishes for the acolyte seems less necessary. However, if this office were held in conjunction with that of reader it would mean that in most parishes there would be a sufficiency of trained personnel to assist the parish priest in his many tasks. In this country at least, too much has fallen on the shoulders of the clergy alone and, as priests get more and more scarce, there is a strong case for the presence and use of well-trained lay people.

NOTES

1 For texts see *Hippolytus: A Text for Students*, ed. and trans. G. J. Cuming (Nottingham: Grove Books, 1976), pp. 8–13. The 'appointment' of readers and subdeacons is mentioned on a later page.

2 For which see my *Christian Celebration: Understanding the Sacraments* (new edition; London: Geoffrey Chapman, 1993), pp. 145–8.

3 For the text of the prayer see *Notitiae*, 283 (February 1990), 2. It is, of course, in Latin.

Unit 10

TONY ROGERS

RITES OF HEALING: RECONCILIATION, ANOINTING, FUNERALS

It might seem rather strange at first sight to see this particular grouping together of rites. What, may one ask, have they got in common? First of all, each of them deals with damage to, or loss of something: baptismal innocence, health, life and relationships. Another common factor which links these rites is that they are concerned with subjects often considered as no-go areas. Sin, sickness and death are all taboo and many of us have great difficulty in facing up to the reality of them in ourselves and in others. Because the Church's liturgical rites focus on the activity of Christ in our lives, perhaps another title which could link reconciliation, anointing and funerals is 'rites of restoration'.

The sacrament of penance deals with the realities of God's mercy and call to ourselves and to others. It also shows the role of the Church in healing the wounds caused by sin and division. The anointing of the sick is concerned with sickness and its implications: the weakness not only of the human body, but also of our spirit and sometimes of our faith. The 'danger of death' factor is always present here, even though frequently that danger is fairly remote. The Order of Christian Funerals deals with the reality of death and acknowledges that there is usually unfinished business for the deceased and/or for the mourners.

The rites of the Church, through words and music, sign and symbol, help the individual and the community come to terms with, accept and cope with serious events. In OCF 4 we read: 'The Church also ministers to the sorrowing and consoles them in the funeral rites with the comforting Word of God and the sacrament of the eucharist.' And again, OCF 9 speaks of the community's role in consoling the mourners: 'The responsibility of ministry of consolation rests with the believing community which heeds the words and example of the Lord Jesus: "Blessed are they who mourn; they shall be consoled" (Matthew 5:3).

170

Each Christian shares in the ministry according to the various gifts and offices of the Church.'

In the General Introduction to *Anointing and Pastoral Care of the Sick* (1972) attention is drawn to the fact that the Church's ministry extends far beyond the confines of a liturgical rite. In APCS 32 and 33 we read:

> If one member suffers in the Body of Christ, which is the
> Church, all members suffer with that member (1 Corinthians
> 12:26). For this reason kindness shown toward the sick and
> works of charity and mutual help for the relief of every kind
> of human want are held in special honour. Every scientific effort
> to prolong life and every act of care for the sick, on the part
> of any person may be considered a proclamation of the Gospel
> and a sharing in Christ's life ministry.
>
> It is thus specially fitting that all baptised Christians share in
> the ministry of mutual charity within the Body of Christ by
> doing all that they can to help the sick return to health,
> by showing love for the sick, and by celebrating the sacraments
> with them.

Music fulfils different roles at different times. For example, in the sacrament of penance suitable music played in the background while individuals await their turn can be a valuable addition to reflection. At the time of death suitable words are often difficult to find. OCF 30 speaks of music allowing 'the community to express convictions and feelings that words alone may fail to convey'. Furthermore, 'it has the power to console and uplift the mourners and to strengthen the unity of the assembly in faith and love'.

The liturgical environment should also be prepared for the rite to be celebrated. The very phrase 'reconciliation room/chapel' conveys both a sense of space and a setting in which reconciliation has pre-eminence over everything else. For some penitents, though, the option to use an old confessional which has not been altered is important. Likewise the body of a deceased Christian is treated with great reverence in the funeral rites. A proper space and setting should therefore be created to ensure that this dignity is truly respected.

Penance

While the eucharist will be at the heart of the worshipping experience of all active Catholics, the same cannot be said of the sacrament of penance. Nonetheless, Christ began his preaching with a call to repentance, as had John the Baptist and the prophets before him. Early Christians, conscious of their high calling, were reluctant to impart absolution to those who had fallen from baptismal grace, but by the third century there was a pastoral move to allow those guilty of serious sin (apostasy, murder and adultery) to be admitted as penitents. This would involve the sinners presenting themselves before the bishop, acknowledging their sin and receiving from him a penance, which often lasted many years or even a lifetime. The season of Lent, originally a time of preparation for those seeking baptism, gradually became more penitential in character, with texts appropriate for penitents being incorporated into the liturgy. So the climax of this penitential period was the forty days of Lent, at the end of which, on Maundy Thursday, the penitents were reconciled and admitted again to the eucharist.

While the early Christians needed to demonstrate to the pagan world that baptism was no easy option but demanded a high standard of moral behaviour for the rest of one's life, there were, however, enormous practical difficulties. Conscious of these demands, many who were sympathetic to Christianity, and were indeed believers at heart, vowed to postpone baptism till their deathbed so that there would be little or no chance of falling from baptismal grace. But life, then as now, was never so predictable, and although there were no cars to run them over, sudden and unexpected death was always possible. For those who had been baptized and found themselves in the order of penitents, a lifetime's penance or a series of consecutive 'sentences' made the sacramental life of many people almost impossible.

It was the seventh-century Irish monks who broke the mould. The monastic practice of the regular 'chapter of faults' was merely a step away from individual confession of sin. Documentary evidence from Ireland and the Anglo-Saxon world shows the 'tariff' system of penances imposed to fit the crime. Initially these penances, much more manageable than the current Roman practice, had to be performed before absolution was given, but eventually, despite resistance from the authorities, the process was reversed with the result that, by the twelfth century, private confession was the norm. The Fourth Lateran Council in 1215 codified this practice, which was further modified by the Council of Trent.

So any Catholic living before Vatican II would have experienced the sacrament only in a private form, and often within the framework of a minimum requirement (the so-called 'Easter duties'). The Constitution on the Liturgy asked that 'the rite and formulas for the sacrament of penance ... be revised so that they give more luminous expression to both the nature and effect of the sacrament' (SC 72).

The Order of Penance was published in 1973 with a strong emphasis on reconciliation, both with God and the Church:

> By the hidden and loving mystery of God's design men are joined together in the bonds of supernatural solidarity, so much so that the sin of one harms the others, just as the holiness of one benefits the others. Penance always entails reconciliation with our brothers and sisters who are always harmed by our sins. (OP 5)

The confession of an individual's sin is still a requirement for the sacrament, though within the context of an inner conversion that prompts that confession:

> we can only approach the kingdom of Christ by metanoia. This is a profound change of the whole person by which one begins to consider, judge and arrange his life according to the holiness and love of God, made manifest in his Son ... The genuineness of penance depends on this heartfelt contrition. For conversion should affect a person from within so that it may progressively enlighten him and render him continually more like Christ. (OP 6a)

The Order provides three forms of the celebration of penance.

1. RECONCILIATION FOR INDIVIDUAL PENITENTS (RITE I). Many churches have adapted existing confessionals to become 'reconciliation rooms'. In effect these small rooms are the place (or chapel) set aside for the celebration of this sacrament alone. As well as giving the penitent the option of sitting opposite the priest or using a grille, this room should speak of what it sets out to do: 'privacy is essential, both visually and acoustically, and both lighting and decoration should be in keeping with the nature of the rite' (Bishops' Conference of England and Wales, *The Parish Church* (CTS, 1984), p. 111). An open Bible (which will be used), a crucifix, icon(s) and candle will all contribute to this particular liturgical environment.

As with all sacramental rites, there is a greeting: 'The priest should welcome the penitent with fraternal charity, and if the occasion permits, address him with friendly words' (OP 16). He then encourages the penitent to trust in God and, after a reading from Scripture, the penitent gives an indication of his/her own circumstances (to help the priest in whatever counsel may be offered subsequently), confesses his/her sins and seeks reconciliation. The priest then gives advice and imposes a penance 'which is not to be thought of simply as an expiation for past sins, but as a help in starting a new life and a remedy for his/her weakness' (OP 18). He pronounces absolution and the rite ends with a short thanksgiving.

2. THE RECONCILIATION OF A GROUP OF PENITENTS WITH INDIVIDUAL CONFESSION AND ABSOLUTION (RITE II). This takes the form of a celebration of the Word – readings, hymns, prayers, homily and an examination of conscience, followed by a call to repentance. After this, private confession and reconciliation follow and the rite concludes with a short thanksgiving.

3. THE RECONCILIATION OF A GROUP OF PENITENTS WITH GENERAL CONFESSION AND ABSOLUTION (RITE III). This follows the same pattern as Rite II, but concludes not with individual confession and reconciliation, but with a prayer of absolution which ends with the formula 'I absolve you . . .'. This form may be used in certain circumstances; e.g. when there is danger of imminent death (a field of battle) or when, despite all reasonable efforts to secure sufficient confessors for the occasion, the number of penitents is too great for them to be able to deal adequately with everyone. In such cases the penitents are required to present themselves within a reasonable time for confession of any grave sins.

In addition to rites of reconciliation, provision is also made for what are called 'penitential celebrations' – similar in structure to Rites II and III above, but without confession or absolution. The Order of Penance sees them as 'offering help in reaching that perfect contrition which comes from charity and enables the faithful to attain God's grace through a desire for the sacrament of penance' (OP 37). It is, however, fair to say that these services are not in widespread use.

Anointing and Pastoral Care of the Sick

We tend to think that because the letter of James (5:14–15) speaks of calling for the priests of the Church to lay hands on the sick and anoint them with oil – for salvation and for healing – that this has been the practice from apostolic times. Certainly the episcopal, priestly and diaconal care of the sick was always a pastoral priority, but it is not until the *Apostolic Tradition* of Hippolytus of Rome (early third century) that we find reference to oil being brought by the faithful to be blessed at the end of the Eucharistic Prayer so that it could be taken home and used when necessary by anyone. The prayer of blessing at the offering of oil is interesting because it is replete with medical overtones, reflecting an era when oil was used as a universal medication:

O God by sanctifying this oil you give holiness to those who use and receive it. With it you anointed kings and priests and prophets. May it likewise now give solace to those who taste it and health to those who use it.

Just over a hundred years later the Sacramentary of Serapion speaks of oil dispelling evil, for physical sickness, sin and evil were closely associated:

Give these creatures [oil and water] the power to heal,
let them drive out every fever, every demon and every sickness.
Let them become for those who use them
a healing and reviving remedy
in the name of your only-begotten Son, Jesus Christ.

There is at this stage neither ritual nor restrictions as to the use of oil. It could be applied as a liniment or taken internally. It was used both in time of serious illness and for minor ailments. It could be repeated as long as the illness persisted, in much the same way as current medical products are accompanied by advice as to dosage. The liturgy, insofar as there was any, took the form of the blessing of the oil, not the anointing itself.

Until the eighth century, although oil was blessed by the bishop, it could be used by all the faithful, despite the apparent restrictions in James 5. Anointing by priests became more widespread, but existed alongside that by lay people until the reforms during the reign of Charlemagne. These resulted in a drastic change (in a short space of time) whereby informal anointing was replaced by 'extreme unction' for those close to death. This took place in the context of a formal ritual celebrated only by bishops and priests. It was at this point that it took on its strongly penitential tone with the anointing of separate senses to remove sins committed by those senses. While this practice may seem, at first sight, a step backwards, it should be remembered that it was part of a move to combat the rise of superstitious practices that had occurred in the wake of the collapse of the Roman Empire. The Carolingian reform represented an attempt to replace the attractions of magic and sorcery with a relatively simple inclusion of texts for anointing into those already in use for the pastoral care of the sick. Irish monks had taken the lead in the practice of individual – and oft repeated – reconciliation while the rest of Europe continued the practice of once-only deathbed reconciliation. So in practice, because the sacraments were only available to those who were reconciled, anointings came close to death, rather than in time of sickness.

The practice of the mediaeval Church, supported by the writings of Thomas Aquinas, Albert the Great, Bonaventure and Duns Scotus, was of a sacrament priestly in character (with no participation on the part of anyone), restricted to proximate and almost certain death and with effects that were seen in spiritual (i.e. forgiveness of sins) rather than physical (i.e. healing) terms. But strangely enough, although the practice of 'extreme unction' persisted up to the reforms of Vatican II (and beyond), the Council of Trent did not endorse the scholastic view of the sacrament for the dying. They spoke of the sick rather than the dying, and described the strengthening of the whole person as its effects. Although the rigorist view of the high Middle Ages was not officially endorsed by Trent, the practice of extreme unction still tended, with minor modifications, to persist down to recent years. The need for 'proximate' danger of death was relaxed, and writers spoke of 'remote' danger instead; it would also help if the sacrament was administered while the sick person was still conscious, and it could be repeated if necessary. Historical research was able to separate the anointing of the sick and dying from the sacrament of penance, despite the link in the minds of many people, even to this day, who speak of 'the last rites'. The anointing of the sick is seen as a sacrament for the restoration of health within the plan and purpose of God.

In 1972 *Anointing and Pastoral Care of the Sick* (APCS) was published, making clear that this is not a sacrament for those 'in extremis' but for those whose health is seriously impaired by sickness and old age. The principles underlying the reform of the sacrament are set out in the Constitution on the Liturgy which says:

> 'Extreme unction', which may also and more fittingly be called 'anointing of the sick', is not a sacrament only for those who are at the point of death. Hence as soon as one of the faithful begins to be in danger of death from sickness or old age, the appropriate time for him to receive the sacrament has already arrived. (SC 73)

Paul VI in the Apostolic Constitution preceding *Pastoral Care of the Sick: Rites of Anointing and Viaticum* sets the sacrament in its dominical and scriptural context, citing the text of James 5. He also gives an historical outline of the sacrament and speaks of the need for reform.

But it is the General Introduction which deals with 'human sickness and its meaning in the mystery of salvation'. It recognizes that suffering and illness are always a problem for human beings; stresses that Christ's love for the sick shows that 'sickness has meaning and value for salvation'; explodes the common myth that sickness is a punishment for sin (John 9:3); and recognizes the tension between fighting 'strenuously against all sickness and being prepared to fill up what is lacking in Christ's sufferings for the salvation of the world'. The notion of ministry to the sick is extended to all who have care of them professionally or personally (APCS 1–4).

'Sickness means that those who are seriously ill need the special help of God's grace in this time of anxiety, lest they be broken in spirit ... and perhaps weakened in their faith' (APCS 5). Because illness can damage body, mind and spirit, the anointing of the sick necessarily combats all negative consequences: it is for the whole person and offers strength in time of temptation, forgiveness of sins and 'grace both to bear and fight pain'. James the apostle speaks of 'the prayer of faith' saving the sick person, and the faith spoken of is to be found in the minister, the recipient and the whole Church.

There are three categories of individuals considered suitable candidates for the anointing of the sick: those whose condition (especially prior to surgery) would give cause for concern; those who by reason of age are experiencing a weakening of body, mind and spirit; and those children who 'have sufficient use of reason' (rather than those who have reached the 'age of reason') to understand the sacrament. But sacraments are for the living, and the dead should not be anointed unless there is uncertainty about the fact of death.

Anointing and Pastoral Care of the Sick provides more than the rite of anointing itself. Of importance too are the pastoral offices involving visits to the sick and dying as well as viaticum – the food for the journey – which may be given by a priest, deacon or special minister of the eucharist.

Undoubtedly this is a sacrament that has been brought out of the intensive care unit or away from the deathbed. Many parishes and pilgrimages will have a regular public and communal celebration of the sacrament during Mass. This can only help to remove the element of fear or terror associated with impending death. The fact that we, like James, can testify that the sick do recover means that, in our own consciousness, we have moved from the concept of a sacrament which sent people on their way ready to meet their maker, to one that brings life and health.

Order of Christian Funerals

Christian burial, affirming resurrection hope from the beginning, developed customs which have persisted, to a great extent, to the present day. But burial rites needed to be markedly different from contemporary pagan practices. For example, while pagans buried their dead by night, the interment of a Christian took place in daylight. The ritual from death to burial took the following pattern. Prayers were said in the home of the deceased, during which the body was washed, anointed and clothed in white. A procession followed, with mourners clad in the white robes of victory, bearing palms, lights and incense, and singing songs of hope. A short office around the body of the deceased brought further comfort to mourners, and during the funeral Mass the sign of peace was given to the deceased as a sign of the union in the Church of living and dead. At burial the custom was to place the body in the grave with feet facing eastward – towards the rising sun, the Sun of righteousness. At specified intervals after burial (the third, ninth and fortieth days) the community would again gather for psalms, hymns and prayers. In the early centuries of the Church's life, peace, hope and trust were the overriding themes in funeral rites.

The mediaeval Church, conscious of human sinfulness (cf. anointing of the sick) and fear of the day of judgement, introduced the absolution after the funeral Mass – demonstrating the power of the priest to forgive sin. Chants such as the *Dies Irae* (originally written for Advent) expressed the consciousness of sin, purgatory and judgement, and texts spoke of the destiny of the soul rather than the whole person. The Roman Ritual of 1614 simplified the funeral rites, which were mainly monastic, for parish use. This, though permitting local variations, was the first worldwide burial rite in the history of the Church. Little changed until the *Ordo Exsequiarum* of 1969, except that cremation was permitted for Catholics from 1965, though without a special rite until 1972.

The Order of Christian Funerals (1990) is still thought by many to be a *new* funeral rite. It is in fact a revision (with new translations) and pastoral adaptation, together with some new material of the *Ordo Exsequiarum* (1969). But it seems to be a new rite, partly because so many of the possibilities offered in the 1969 edition remained hidden treasures, and partly because the current text is arranged in such a way that all possible rites or combination of rites are set out in full. Within the English-speaking world, local conferences of bishops have been able to authorize adaptations of the Roman model, to suit particular regional and cultural circumstances. So far, Canada, Ireland, and England, Wales and Scotland have produced their own editions of the Order of Christian Funerals.

It is in the face of one of society's modern taboos – death – that the Church 'confidently proclaims that God created each person for eternal life and that Jesus, the Son of God, by his death and resurrection, has broken the chain of sin and death that bind humanity' (OCF 1). Funerals offer the mourners the chance to hear that truth proclaimed in Scripture, prayer and song, as well as thanking God for the life of the deceased and 'commending them to God's merciful love and pleading for the forgiveness of their sins' (OCF 6).

Death has its repercussions, not only on the immediate family but also on the whole community. St Paul's teaching about the Body of Christ speaks of the effects – good and bad – that the life and death of its members have on one another. Just as we naturally care in time of sickness, so also in death 'the faithful are called to a ministry of consolation to those who have suffered the loss of one whom they love'. A hallmark of the General Introduction is that it is thoroughly pastoral as well as liturgical in character, speaking of the importance of members of the local church community being on hand to assist the family with some of the routine tasks of daily living, as well as supporting them in the funeral rites.

The preparation of the funeral liturgy gives an opportunity for family and friends to be involved in liturgical ministry. Provision is also made for someone other than the priest or deacon to 'speak in memory of the deceased'. The Order of Christian Funerals sees the rites as the way in which the Church accompanies the deceased on their journey to their last resting place and to the Lord, and accompanies the mourners in their grief. To underline the fact that this is a process that begins before death and continues beyond burial or cremation, there are a series of rites – some informal, others more ritualistic in character. They are divided as follows:

1. PRE-FUNERAL RITES AND PRAYERS:
   (a) Prayers after death, and on the occasion when the family first gathers around the body.
   (b) Vigil for the deceased – with or without the reception of the body in church.
   (c) A simple form of reception in church, and a short rite when the family gathers prior to the transfer of the body to the church or place of committal.

2. THE FUNERAL LITURGY – normally a Mass, but on occasions a funeral liturgy outside Mass.

3. RITE OF COMMITTAL at a graveside or in a crematorium; for occasions immediately following a funeral liturgy, or when there has been a delay, or when no funeral liturgy has preceded. A short rite for the burial of ashes is also provided.

These rites are replicated for children, with the addition of a short liturgy of commendation suitable after miscarriage, stillbirth or neonatal death. Special provision is made for the adaptations needed for the funeral of catechumens who, though unbaptized, are part of 'the household of Christ'. A model for Morning and Evening Prayer is provided as well as a large corpus of prayers which are suitable for particular persons (husband, wife, bishop, elderly, young) or for circumstances of death (long illness, violent death, suicide). These can be used at any point when a collect-type prayer is appropriate.

The pastoral adaptations for England, Wales and Scotland have taken into account the rapidly changing circumstances of religious life and practice in Great Britain. The increased proportion of committals that take place at a crematorium, together with the need for a 'one-stop' liturgy – regrettable in many ways but a necessary response to deal with those funerals which are arranged without prior reference to the local priest, but which call for a Catholic presence at a cemetery or crematorium chapel – are catered for in the Order of Christian Funerals. The Irish and Canadian editions have made pastoral adaptations to suit their circumstances.

Careful study of the General Introduction, the pastoral notes which accompany each section of the rites and the texts themselves, will show that while planning and understanding are a vital ingredient for all involved in this ministry of consolation, great flexibility is possible and sensitivity necessary in situations where the Church must respond quickly and compassionately.

DOCUMENTATION AND BIBLIOGRAPHY

Order of Christian Funerals (London: Geoffrey Chapman, 1991), General Introduction and Pastoral Notes.
Pastoral Care of the Sick (London: Geoffrey Chapman, 1983), Apostolic Constitution and Introductions.
The Rite of Penance (London: Collins/Goodliffe Neale, 1976), Introduction.
Tom Coyle (ed.), *Christian Ministry to the Sick* (London: Geoffrey Chapman, 1986).
J. D. Crichton, *Christian Celebration: Understanding the Sacraments* (new edition; London: Geoffrey Chapman, 1993), chs 9, 10 and 11.
Stephen Dean (ed.), *The Parish Funeral* (Great Wakering: McCrimmons, 1991).
D. A. Withey, *Catholic Worship* (Bury St Edmunds: Kevin Mayhew, 1990), ch. 15.